Toward
Successful
SCHOOL
CRISIS
Intervention

To all those who have suffered from misfortune

Toward
Successful
SCHOOL
CRISIS
Intervention

9 Nine
Key
Issues

Charles M. Jaksec III

CORWIN PRESS
A SAGE Publications Company
Thousand Oaks, CA 91320

For information:

Corwin Press
A Sage Publications Company
2455 Teller Road
Thousand Oaks, California 91320
www.corwinpress.com

Sage Publications Ltd.
1 Oliver's Yard
55 City Road
London EC1Y 1SP
United Kingdom

Sage Publications India Pvt. Ltd.
B 1/I 1 Mohan Cooperative
  Industrial Area
Mathura Road, New Delhi 110 044
India

Sage Publications Asia-Pacific Pte. Ltd.
33 Pekin Street #02-01
Far East Square
Singapore 048763

Printed in the United States of America

Library of Congress Cataloging-in-Publication Data

Jaksec, Charles M.
Toward successful school crisis intervention: 9 key issues/
Charles M. Jaksec III.
    p. cm.
Includes bibliographical references
ISBN 978-1-4129-4887-6 (cloth)
ISBN 978-1-4129-4888-3 (pbk.)
    1. School crisis management. I. Title.

LB2866.5.J35 2007
371.7'13—dc22

2006102696

This book is printed on acid-free paper.

07 08 09 10 11 12   10 9 8 7 6 5 4 3 2 1

Acquisitions Editor:	Stacy Wagner
Editorial Assistant:	Joanna Coelho
Production Editor:	Denise Santoyo
Copy Editor:	Trey Thoelke
Typesetter:	C&M Digitals (P) Ltd.
Cover Designer:	Scott Van Atta
Graphic Designer:	Lisa Riley

Contents

Acknowledgments

I would like to thank my colleagues on the Hillsborough County School District's Crisis Intervention Team. Their support and expertise have been invaluable. I would also like to acknowledge my mentor in the field of crisis intervention, Dr. Richard Weinberg.

I have drawn inspiration from Dr. Ofra Ayalon, with whom I've had the privilege of discussing school crisis intervention through the years. She has selflessly helped countless children around our world live peacefully during turbulent times. Dr. Ayalon's legendary status in the field of crisis intervention is richly deserved.

Stacy Wagner, Acquisitions Editor at Corwin Press, has provided hours of guidance during the completion of this book. Her talent and patience were necessary and truly appreciated. Joanna Coelho and Denise Santoyo, at Corwin also provided much-needed assistance with this book and I value their support.

My mother, Marie Jaksec, has always been a great source of support for me, as are my brothers and friends, such as Kenny Karekos, Ryan Holden, Mark "Pete" Peterson, Kathy Toler, Dr. Joe Brown, and Tim Matthew.

To Samantha, Jordan, and Rockie, I love you more than you will ever know.

Finally, and most important, thank you Jesus, Mary, Joseph, and Jude.

Corwin Press wishes to thank the following peer reviewers for their editorial insight and guidance:

Sharie Blankenship, LPC, NCC, NBCT, School Counselor
Ardmore High School, Ardmore, OK

Carol J. Lark, Superintendent
Douglas County School District, Minden, NV

Cheri Lovre, Director
Crisis Management Institute, Salem, OR

Marla W. McGhee, Associate Professor of Educational
   Leadership
Texas State University–San Marcos, TX

Michael Pines, Consultant
School of Mental Health/Crisis Intervention,
Los Angeles County Office of Education, Los Angeles, CA

Sharon R. Roemer, Principal
Ocean View Elementary School, Arroyo Grande, CA

Carrie Wachter, Assistant Professor of School Counseling
Department of Educational Studies, Purdue University, West
   Lafayette, IN

Bill Walsh, School Counselor
New Fairfield High School, New Fairfield, CT

About the Author

Chuck Jaksec has been employed as a school social worker in the Hillsborough County School District for 21 years. He has also been a member of the district's crisis intervention team for 18 years. He is currently the chairperson of the district's Bullying Committee and is a member of the District's Violence Prevention Committee.

Jaksec received a BS in Social Work from Slippery Rock University of Pennsylvania (1980), an MA in Counseling Services from Slippery Rock University (1982), an EdS in Counselor Education from the University of South Florida (1991), and a PhD in Curriculum and Instruction from the University of South Florida in (1996).

Jaksec's other published books include *The Confrontational Parent: A Practical Guide for School Leaders* (2003) and *The Difficult Parent: An Educator's Guide to Handling Aggressive Behaviors* (2004). He speaks nationally and locally on the topics of school crisis intervention and parental aggression toward school personnel. He is married to Samantha Jaksec, a reading consultant with the Florida Diagnostic and Learning Resources System. They are the parents of Jordan and Michael.

Introduction

As a district crisis intervention team member for 18 years, I have had the opportunity to assist and support students and faculty members during times of crisis, including suicide, homicide, and accidental, natural, or man-made tragedies. From events that had a relatively small impact on a school population, such as a classmate's illness, to the school-wide reaction witnessed during the events of September 11, 2001, my opportunities to observe and attempt to stabilize school populations have always proven both challenging and rewarding.

I have written *Toward Successful School Crisis Intervention: 9 Key Issues* with the intention of addressing several specific topics that might occasionally cause school staff serving on crisis intervention teams—whom I'll refer to as *interventionists*—to question their methods, effectiveness, or overall direction. Optimally, the identification and examination of these issues, coupled with suggestions and alternative options, will result in a more comprehensive and effective crisis intervention effort.

Toward Successful School Crisis Intervention is not intended to be a compendium of crisis intervention research, a "cookbook" for intervening during crises, or simply my memoirs as a seasoned school crisis interventionist. Rather, it brings together relevant research with my own recommendations based on both the oversights and successes of school crisis intervention teams. In a head-on manner, this book identifies areas that have been traditionally overlooked, or existed as sensitive subject matter in the area of school crisis intervention.

Each chapter—framed as an *issue* that is key to successful intervention—contains vignettes, helpful tips, and discussion questions that will allow you to gain a greater understanding of issues related to school crisis intervention efforts. Ideally used in study groups of crisis intervention team members, this book will encourage reflection and help teams organize and plan, as best they can, in advance of crises.

Issue One: The Responsibility for School Crisis Intervention: Whose Job Is This, Anyway? addresses the important question of which school personnel should actually carry out the task of crisis intervention. Possible reasons for hesitancy or refusal to become involved in crisis intervention efforts are also discussed.

Issue Two: Necessary Attributes and Abilities for Team Members: What Does It Take? focuses on the personal qualities and abilities that those who become members of the school crisis intervention team should possess in order to best serve the school populations that they are called on to assist.

Issue Three: Training of School Crisis Intervention Team Members: Going to War Without a Weapon? examines the effects of inadequate training for school crisis interventionists and their ramifications on students, fellow crisis interventionists, staff members, and the reputation of both school and community. The chapter also addresses the degree to which various professionals on intervention teams (e.g., counselors and psychologists) are trained in graduate school, and makes recommendations for ongoing, inservice professional development.

Issue Four: Logistical School Crisis Response: The Overlooked Intervention, or the physical movement of students and staff during a crisis, is often overlooked in lieu of psychological crisis intervention efforts. Specific personnel involved in logistical crisis response and issues involved in its implementation are also discussed.

Issue Five: Determining the Impact of a Crisis: How Big Will the Bang Be? allows the interventionist to consider several variables that might help determine the impact that a crisis might have on a school population. The benefits of assessing these variables are identified.

Issue Six: Non-School-Based Crisis Intervention Teams: Districts and Schools Working Together discusses the value of non-school-based support teams, widely held perceptions of these teams, and their relationships with existing school-based crisis intervention teams and these non-school-based teams.

Issue Seven: Teachers: The Overlooked Interventionists provides an opportunity to consider the role of the classroom teacher as crisis interventionist. The advantages of teacher support in the classroom setting are also detailed.

Issue Eight: Did We Forget Anyone? Addressing the Needs of Every Staff Member focuses on a variety of reasons why staff members occasionally fail to receive crisis intervention support, and how schools can ensure that everyone receives appropriate attention.

Issue Nine: Primary Prevention: Preparing for Crises Before They Happen offers a look at a unique type of crisis intervention that prepares students to deal with their emotions before a crisis takes place. Although considered unorthodox by some, it can be an effective means of support for school populations. The reactive tendency of most intervention efforts is examined, and the case is made for the timeliness and importance of engaging in primary prevention.

During an interview, a reporter once asked me if the rigors of crisis intervention ever "took a toll." I explained that during times of misfortune, individuals can understandably descend to really low points in their lives, for some *the* lowest point. It is in assisting in their recovery that I find tremendous gratification. It's not the toll that the situation exacts, but rather, the fulfillment that the intervention offers. I hope that *Toward Successful School Crisis Intervention* will help school crisis interventionists experience a higher degree of satisfaction as they provide their valuable service on our nation's campuses.

The Responsibility for School Crisis Intervention

Whose Job Is This, Anyway?

Early Friday morning, Sheila Andrews, a second-year principal at Marden Elementary School, hears police sirens outside her school. As she hurries toward the front of the building, a frantic parent notifies her that a fourth-grade student has just been the victim of an attempted abduction. Fortunately, a police officer was summoned by an adult crossing guard, and an arrest is being made. Several other officers responded and assisted with the arrest.

Although the student was safe, the attempted abduction and subsequent chaos occurred in full view of approximately 150 students who had congregated before school on the playground. The majority of the students are visibly shaken. Three hysterical students have been brought to the nurse's office due to painful eye irritation as the result of the pepper spray used by the police officers. Teachers have already begun requesting assistance because their students are extremely upset.

After contacting district officials, Principal Andrews meets with several staff members whom she selected to provide crisis support. The assistant principal immediately begins to cry, as the victim is one of her student assistants. She appears upset and unable to take the lead as planned. The principal relates her concern that many students have witnessed the incident and crisis intervention may be warranted. She now looks to her first-year guidance counselor to spearhead the crisis intervention efforts, but is shocked to hear the counselor comment, "I'm not really comfortable in situations like this." The school psychologist has 20 years of experience but little crisis intervention training. Though he is very willing to become involved, Principal Andrews is not comfortable with the school psychologist's skill level in the area of crisis intervention. During a crisis the previous year, his overexuberance interfered with the provision of services.

As the morning progresses, Principal Andrews is relieved that her school has stabilized due to the timely arrival of two guidance counselors, a social worker, and a human relations specialist from a neighboring middle school. At the conclusion of the long day, she consults with her general director and notes that the student population was at a disadvantage during the incident due to her staff's hesitation, refusal, or inability to provide crisis intervention services.

School districts differ in regard to how they define crisis intervention procedures. Ideally, the district will detail procedures and provide district-level support. Some districts have school-based crisis intervention teams to provide physical safety and psychological support to students. These teams might be responsible for on-site planning for crisis response or members might be involved on a crisis planning team. Districts probably won't specify size or membership, but will cite the need for various staff to participate on the team (e.g., school nurse, school psychologist, teachers). The responsibility for the crisis intervention team ultimately falls to the school to develop its own specific plan and to identify personnel who will conduct crisis intervention activities. School administrators often assume the task of planning and identifying crisis intervention duties.

Before we examine the intricacies of crisis intervention, let's look at a most basic question: "Within a school setting, who should actually be required to provide crisis intervention services?" Some staff members might respond, "We all should! It's our responsibility!" Others might answer, "I would be willing to provide crisis intervention, if I knew it was one of my duties and I had adequate training." Still others could opine, "Crisis intervention just isn't my job." As these responses reflect, the simple question, "Who should provide crisis intervention?" often presents a lot of confusion.

WHO SHOULD PROVIDE CRISIS INTERVENTION?

Optimally, all school personnel would share a sense of responsibility regarding the provision of support during a crisis, but, unfortunately, this isn't always the case. Hesitation is often evident and the question remains: "Is school crisis intervention actually every staff member's responsibility?" It seems that two separate positions are prevalent regarding this important issue. One camp steadfastly maintains that all school personnel are indeed obliged to render support during a crisis-related event. Using a somewhat dramatic analogy, if an Army platoon comes under attack, all of the soldiers within that platoon, whether rifleman, medic, cook, or communications officer, take up arms to defend their position. There is no consideration that "This isn't really my job!" On the other hand, there are those who feel that, regardless of their position, they cannot be forced to become involved in such an intense task as crisis intervention. As one teacher explained, "I don't ask you to teach, so please don't expect me to do crisis intervention."

It's also understandable that one's position in a school might play a big role in predicting willingness to become involved in crisis support efforts. For instance, it would be reasonable to assume that a seasoned guidance counselor might be more equipped to become involved in the provision of crisis intervention services than a first-year teacher or librarian who has never been exposed to a schoolwide crisis. (Of course this is not to say that the aforementioned individuals might not be more than willing and able to play a critical role during a school crisis.) Although it is typically the school's responsibility to put together its own team, the team's functions are often dictated by district policy and predetermined procedures. According to the Center for Mental Health in Schools at UCLA (2005), "In most instances, the district's administration will have provided the school with detailed guidelines for handling major disasters during the emergency itself and in the immediate aftermath" (p. 6).

Not surprisingly, the more detailed a district plan is, the more likely the school-based crisis intervention team is to feel comfortable and confident in its abilities to provide services to students. If a principal or site administrator establishes a "schoolwide support" mentality regarding crisis response and makes clear the value of the crisis team, then team members will in all likelihood be well aware of the expectations placed on them when a crisis does occur. As is so often the case, the attitude that comes from the top down has much influence over the effectiveness of those "on the ground."

No school can afford not to respond to a crisis, and so a carefully selected, diverse, and well-prepared intervention team is critical to creating safe and healthy schools.

REASONS FOR RELUCTANCE

Why are some staff members more than willing to become involved in crisis intervention efforts whereas other staff members remain reticent and uncomfortable during these situations? Let's look at five reasons why staff members might hesitate to become involved in crisis intervention efforts.

1. Crisis Intervention Is an Intimidating Task

This point almost goes without saying, but it's nevertheless an important one to keep in mind. Crises occur on different magnitudes, and we all have a level of comfort that varies depending on the circumstance. Crises can be situational (such as an earthquake) or developmental (such as when adults experience what's commonly known as a *midlife crisis*). We typically and understandably associate crises with negative events, such as death, injury, disaster, or accident. On occasion, a seemingly positive event can lead to an emotional crisis in a student's life, as with a parent's remarriage or job relocation. These events can all have a dramatic impact on students, and possibly trigger a crisis during school hours.

Some faculty members have no desire to be in the middle of a hurricane in which little good is blowing. Are these individuals wrong when they hesitate or even refuse to participate in intervention efforts? Of course not. Crises can be intimidating, no matter the scale. Yet while some people avoid participation or involvement in relief efforts, others seem to be drawn to these situations, possessing a "help at all cost" attitude.

An interventionist's first assignments or "call outs" in a crisis can be very unsettling. Though it's difficult to be comfortable while others are experiencing misfortune, this "scariness" or discomfort can be diminished to some extent through adequate training and experience. The acquisition of both can greatly increase confidence when the call for assistance comes.

2. Crisis Intervention May Not Be in the Staff Member's Job Description

Very often, crisis intervention duties are not included in the job descriptions of most types of school personnel. However, the majority of school-based personnel can assist in some manner during crisis responses. For example, though guidance counselors, school psychologists, and school social workers traditionally play a major role during crisis situations—especially in the areas of crisis counseling—I've also witnessed janitors arranging rooms for impromptu counseling sessions, cafeteria workers providing much needed refreshment for the exhausted, office personnel directing "traffic" as students descend on guidance suites, nurses providing medical attention, and school resource officers securing campus perimeters. A crisis counseling component may not be evident in every job description, but most staff members do have an opportunity to provide valuable support in some manner. Some principals demand that all staff be involved in a crisis response, and other administrators choose to let a specialized team of interventionists address the needs in their schools. Regardless of each school's expectations, it is imperative that every staff member knows what his or her responsibility is in relation to crisis-related events. This awareness can only serve to prevent confusion when the unfortunate occurs.

3. Many Staff Members Lack Knowledge About Crisis Intervention

Talented interventionists can provide effective support because they are secure in their knowledge of crisis response. As a result, they can effectively offer "psychological first aid"—that is, mental health services to help address upsetting psychological reactions and "create and sustain an environment of (1) safety, (2) calming, (3) connectedness to others, (4) self-efficacy—or empowerment, and (5) hopefulness"—during and in the aftermath of a crisis (Center for Mental Health in Schools at UCLA, 2005).

Conversely, a lack of knowledge in the area of crisis intervention can work against school personnel by weakening their self-assurance. The intensity of a crisis coupled with a dearth of knowledge in the provision of support can understandably deter staff members from wanting to become involved in intervention efforts. Becoming well versed in the area of school crisis intervention first requires the acquisition of training, and then, actual experience. "Getting your feet wet" goes a long way toward improving how response procedures are implemented, and in turn, these experiences go a long way toward building skill and maintaining poise.

4. Past Negative Experience May Affect Willingness to Get Involved

It is human nature to shy away from something that, on first experience, proved negative. For example, at an early age, a bad first visit to the dentist's office can set the stage for years of trepidation when toothaches occur and another appointment is necessary. Likewise, when school personnel become involved in a crisis response, a poor first experience might prevent them from being willing to become involved in subsequent interventions.

Few experienced crisis interventionists have ever applied their skills without being challenged. What makes these interventionists want to continue to provide crisis intervention? Interestingly, they'll reason that for every bad situation there are five good experiences where their presence made a real difference. It's important to identify the negative experiences immediately following those interventions and this is usually done in debriefings sessions. According to Jimerson, Brock, and Pletcher (2005), once the crisis response is over,

> It is critical to ensure that all team members are given the opportunity to debrief. The primary goal of such activities is to ensure that crisis response teams are successfully able to return to their pre-crisis roles and responsibilities. In addition, it is important to recognize that every crisis response is a learning experience. (p. 287)

Any problems or concerns can be dealt with immediately and as a result, the interventionist's negative attitude toward crisis support might be altered.

5. Liability Issues Are a Genuine Concern

The possibility of saying or doing the "wrong thing," and its repercussions, is a legitimate issue for many teachers, counselors, psychologists, and others who may be involved in the intervention effort. Liability issues can be a real concern, but staff members who have been adequately trained in crisis intervention rarely voice this sentiment. This serves to underscore the importance of adequate and ongoing inservice training.

There is an extensive body of literature on crisis intervention strategies and techniques that has come out of school psychology (Brock, Sandoval, & Lewis, 2001; James & Gilliland, 2004; Pitcher & Poland, 1992; Roberts, 2005; Sandoval, 2001), but schoolwide training for all professionals involved in crisis intervention efforts is critical if school staff are to knowledgably come together and act during crises.

Nevertheless, we might emphasize that tens of thousands of students and staff members are assisted each year in our nation's schools with a paucity of subsequent legal actions. According to Zirkel and Gluckman (1996), the key is to remain sensible. Becoming paralyzed by or paranoid from the fear of liability can be educationally and professionally damning.

EAGER TO HELP BUT UNPREPARED

In contrast to staff members who hesitate or refuse to become involved in crisis intervention efforts are those who are more than willing to lend assistance, but shouldn't be included in the provision of certain services. These eager staff members can be divided into two categories: those adequately trained and experienced in crisis intervention and those, like Martin Thomas, who attempt to render support with little or no training and experience. Let's take a look at Martin's story.

Only Fools Rush In

School social worker Martin Thomas has recently been selected to be a member of his school district's non-school-based crisis intervention team. For years he had desired to participate on a crisis response team and, during a brief interview, Thomas explained to the team's supervisor that he was well versed in intervention techniques and possessed an abundance of crisis-related experience.

After several weeks, Thomas is assigned to a high school where three students had been critically injured in a car accident. It's soon evident that he possesses little knowledge and experience in school crisis intervention. After being asked to conduct small-group counseling in the media center, Thomas accomplishes little during the session and prematurely dismisses 15 students after ten minutes. The students do not return to their classes, disperse throughout the school, and in the process disturb ongoing classes. Thomas proceeds to the guidance suite and informs four female students that they have permission to go home for the day. It is later discovered that these students didn't know the victims and only wished to leave campus. Thomas exits the campus immediately after dismissal, missing the mandated debriefing session. He later explains that he was unaware of the mandate for debriefing.

As evidenced by this example, ill-equipped and overeager members of the crisis intervention team, can interfere on the most basic level with the overall provision of services during the crisis response. They do not have an opportunity to learn "on the job." Some didactic component must be made available before the interventionist can effectively engage in actual crisis intervention services. Are these overly enthusiastic staff members to blame? No. Not even Thomas, who for all intents and purposes lied to the crisis team's supervisor. His qualifications should have been assessed before he was permitted to render services, no matter how eager he appeared or how qualified he said he was. Thomas's inexperience did not have dire effects, but the fact remains that in a very short period, he:

1. Managed to disturb the school environment when he dismissed students prematurely

2. May have placed four students at risk when he permitted them to leave campus

3. Disregarded team policy by not attending the mandated afterschool debriefing session where some of his mistakes could have been identified and possibly remedied

Throughout all of Thomas's oversights and mistakes, the responsibility for his poor performance remained with the individual who actually supervised the crisis team of which he was an active member. Whether superintendent, principal, or crisis team leader, individuals in leadership positions are ultimately responsible for the provision of a thorough training component. Failure to offer adequate training is to invite a new interventionist an opportunity to provide services haphazardly. A thorough training and internship can act as a safeguard through serving to increase the interventionist's knowledge base and exposing the interventionist's weakness and strengths.

Figure 1.1   Roles and Responsibilities of Crisis Intervention Team Members

Role	Responsibility
Crisis Coordinator *Usually the principal or a designee, commonly a school or guidance counselor*	*Oversees crisis intervention activities, i.e., consults with school/district personnel, provides assignments, conducts debriefings*
Medical Liaison	*Provides medical care, consults with other medical personnel (school based/non-school-based)*
Security Liaison, School Resource Officer, or designee	*Secures campus, provides information, addresses volatile individuals*
Media Liaison	*Provides information and conducts interviews with media personnel*
Family/Parent Liaison	*Acts as contact between family and school*
Counseling Liaison	*Coordinates counseling efforts with district-level crisis intervention team*
Campus Liaison	*Communicates the specifics of the crisis to school-based faculty*

SOURCE: Adapted from the School District of Volusia County, *Crisis Intervention Manual*, revised for the 2005/2006 school year, p. 10.

Helpful Tips

- Address the issue of school crisis intervention early in the school year by establishing a "school crisis response team, a team leader, and a crisis response manager" during preplanning staff meetings (Jimerson et al., 2005, p. 280). At the beginning of the school year, staff interest is usually piqued. Establishing a crisis intervention team early in the school year also serves as a safeguard against being unprepared for a crisis that might occur in August or September. Specific training needs should also be addressed at this time.
- Create a visual chart that illustrates crisis intervention responsibilities. This chart should be posted in a highly visible place, such as a teacher work area. Information on this chart should be readily accessible to all faculty and staff.
- Be aware of the issue of liability, but don't let it affect your decision to become involved in crisis intervention. Talk to your administrators and get answers to some of your questions before deciding not to participate on the team.

Questions for Discussion

1. If a crisis situation affected your school today, who would respond? How long did you have to think about your response? If your response took a significant time, maybe this issue should be brought to the attention of the school administration before a crisis occurs.

2. Do you know school personnel who have shied away from crisis intervention? In your opinion, what were the main reasons for their hesitation or refusal? Do you consider their reasons valid?

3. Does the administration at your school consider crisis intervention an important service? If not, how could you play a role in helping the administration look more favorably on the provision of crisis intervention?

Necessary Attributes and Abilities for Team Members

What Does It Take?

*Carol Meadows is a seventh-grade middle school guidance coun-
selor with more than 25 years of experience. She is known as a
fine counselor, but at times she presents herself as an "inflexible
know-it-all," as she was described by a former colleague. Meadows
maintains that she is comfortable with her involvement on the
school's crisis response team, whose members include the school
principal, assistant principal, and school nurse, however, she has
confided to several staff members that she becomes "rattled" in
crisis response situations. In past crises, Meadows has attempted
to refer crisis intervention duties to her colleagues in spite of her
expertise.*

 *Midway through a routine school day, Meadows is notified
by her assistant principal that a sixth-grade boy has had an
epileptic seizure in full view of his classmates. Meadows is the*

only guidance counselor available because her guidance colleague is attending a workshop in a neighboring school district. As she arrives at the room, the teacher and administrators are attempting to remove the students from the classroom and direct them to the cafeteria. As the nurse attends to the student, sirens are heard outside.

When Meadows and several other school personnel arrive in the cafeteria, she notices that most of the 20 students are weeping and asking if their classmate is going to die. As the administrators offer suggestions regarding the seating of the students, Meadows takes charge with little intention of accepting suggestions. To the chagrin of the principal, Meadows displays little patience and empathy toward the students as she attempts to begin a large group discussion. As a result, Meadows experiences great difficulty connecting with the students. After the principal assures the class that their classmate will recover, the administrator continues to attend to the frightened students. Meadows informs the principal that she will remain in the cafeteria as long as necessary, although, she would prefer to see students individually in her office.

Attributes for Handling a Crisis

Have you ever worked with a Carol Meadows? Counselors like Meadows are talented, confident professionals who have done countless students a world of good; however, they do great work only if they are operating within their own parameters. Unfortunately, if their duties are outside of these parameters, they have difficultly working within the framework of the crisis response unit. As competent as Meadows was, she showed little interest in the area of crisis intervention. Ironically, she had steadfastly maintained that crisis intervention presented no problem for her, but it was obvious that she lacked many of the necessary attributes to be an effective crisis interventionist.

What qualities are necessary to engage effectively in crisis intervention? Several attributes will be identified that might help prospective interventionists assess whether they have what it takes to provide effective support during a crisis-related event. It should be emphasized that though staff members might be weak in a certain area (e.g., the ability to work in a chaotic situation), this by no means indicates that they should-n't become involved in the crisis intervention process within their schools. It's amazing what experience, an increase in knowledge, and desensitizing to crisis situations can do to improve or obtain the necessary qualities that are so much a part of the crisis interventionist's makeup.

In no order of importance, let's look at several additional qualities and abilities that members of the crisis intervention team should posses.

Willingness to Learn

It sounds cliché, but no two crises are alike. Every turbulent situation presents a great opportunity to learn and incorporate a host of ways to effectively address the needs of the student and faculty population. Crisis personnel rarely, if ever, reach a point at which they "know it all." Unfortunately, if this mind-set is held by an interventionist or clique within the team, it can become problematic. A team member should never choose his or her personal way of operating in lieu of a predetermined method with which the entire team is familiar. Professionals should take every opportunity to consider new and innovative methods of crisis intervention and maintain a simple willingness to learn. There should never come a time when any one person's way of operating is "gospel" and sug-gestions and recommendations are ignored. This pertains to those professionals involved in either the provision of psy-chological support or the logistical aspects of crisis inter-vention. A willingness to learn is an invaluable quality for all crisis interventionists, whether seasoned veterans or novices.

Courage

One can be trained to learn many skills for effectively intervening during a crisis. However, you may not see other innate attributes on a résumé that can be valuable during a crisis. One attribute that we often fail to consider is courage. Without it, many interventions would be impossible. Most of the crises that impact schools involve a loss of a life, illness, injury, or misfortune that affects any segment of the school population. As a result, students and staff suffer emotionally and/or physically. When individuals are summoned to lend support for these victims, it's often under very trying and turbulent circumstances. School crisis intervention is truly not work for the timid, so becoming involved in this task certainly takes a degree of courage.

My first official "call out" as a crisis intervention team member was due to the suicide of a student, which occurred in a classroom. Talk about a baptism by fire! I recall feeling somewhat scared about what I would witness when arriving at the school and what would transpire during the course of the day. How would the students react? How would I react?

I recall a counselor who actually hid behind her office door in the midst of the chaos to avoid becoming involved in the response. Over the course of her career, this woman had planned many successful programs that had helped our school show evidence of closing the achievement gap. She was incredibly valuable in this regard, but it was clear that her strengths did not lie in crisis intervention. Was that counselor a coward or less professional than anyone else? Certainly not. Nonetheless, it became apparent early in my career that this type of work required exceptional courage and a strong willingness to get involved during very trying times.

Patience

It's safe to say that anyone who has ever worked in a school setting possesses some degree of patience, but we rarely think of patience when we speak of crisis intervention. From the minute services are rendered, any number of situations can test the patience of the most competent of intervention team members, such as:

- Attempting to counsel a student who is intentionally overplaying her emotions in order to receive attention
- Dealing with an administrator who refuses to heed suggestions as students move uncontrolled through the school after a crisis
- Granting an interview to a reporter who has been known to misquote statements

Abilities in Handling a Crisis

A willingness to learn, courage, and patience are all essential qualities that crisis interventionists should have, but several other abilities are equally important for the school crisis interventionist to possess.

Defer to Others With More Expertise

Although almost all types of school personnel can become involved in crisis intervention, it's reasonable to assume that certain types of interventions require more training than others. For example, the provision of psychological support necessitates a greater amount of training than directing a crowd of distraught students to the auditorium.

No matter the level of training necessary or the level of expertise possessed, it's important to realize that regardless of the role one assumes during a crisis, there will invariably come a time when orders must be followed. This could be uncomfortable for an interventionist who is accustomed to being in charge. For instance, if a non-school-based crisis intervention team is summoned to a school, it is imperative for that team to recognize that they are supporting the efforts of that school, not replacing the existing support personnel, if indeed school-based support personnel are in place. (For more information on district-level crisis intervention teams, see Chapter 6.)

Responding teams—whether school-based or not—take on different support roles, and only some of the members will assume positions of leadership.

One's role during a crisis may very well be different than it was during previous crisis responses. Effective administrators remain in charge but still value input from their support personnel, regardless of whether these personnel are school-based or non-school-based. Their attitudes tend to reflect, "You tell me what we need to do to get us through this." There are truly no large egos allowed during a crisis response, and deferring to others is necessary.

Assess Your Emotional and Psychological State Honestly

Whether dealing with a personal loss, relationship issues, or any number of other concerns that can easily affect performance in the work setting, the school crisis interventionist must be cognizant of his or her own mental state. To not be is to risk the quality and effectiveness of the intervention. Even professionals can be unaware of the extent to which their moods or behavior are affected by issues that they may (or may not) be dealing with effectively. The interventionist should also be willing to discuss with superiors the possibility of not being summoned to a school crisis if his or her emotional or physical well-being will be at risk.

According to an article by Chibarro and Jackson (2006), in offering strategies for school counselors to help students cope with terrorism, counselors need to assess their own personal trauma level. If one feels vulnerable under duress, the subsequent ability to work with children is diminished. Chibarro and Jackson also explain that emotional stability is necessary to enable freedom of discussion. The existence of past or present personal issues can be inhibiting. If such is the case, a call for assistance from fellow staff must be made.

Be Flexible, Accessible, and Spontaneous

Our friend Carol Meadows displayed little flexibility. As mentioned previously, crisis intervention is not an exact science and every situation might call for a different plan or action.

Flexibility might be required in the form of working in an unfamiliar school environment or school population, reacting to different types of crises, or assuming different roles during a response. In contrast, rigidity works against the school crisis interventionist mainly because it restricts the scope of his or her talents.

Unfortunately, crises don't come with a place and time of arrival attached. In fact, it seems that they occur when we least expect or are least prepared to deal with them. Whether a secretary is typing the minutes of a meeting, a school psychologist is completing educational testing, a school social worker is getting ready for a important home visit, or a counselor is addressing the needs of a troubled student, the ability to drop everything and begin carrying out the planned steps of crisis intervention is paramount, if a staff member is to be involved in the provision of services. Undoubtedly, the unpredictability of a crisis call can be an inconvenience, but being readily available and respecting one's on-call status makes the process of intervention more manageable for both interventionists and those summoning them to action.

The ability to think on one's feet or improvise is not only handy, but might even be considered a prerequisite for the school crisis interventionist. Turbulent situations seldom offer opportunities for supervisory direction. The need to make quick decisions is common and good judgment a necessity. Improvisation is also required because the nature of crises makes the ability to change direction or modify plans essential. While the necessity of rapid-fire planning, decision making, and improvisation can at times prove to be intimidating, it also makes the endeavor of crisis intervention less stressful.

Work "Above the Fray"

It's essential for the crisis interventionist, especially when assuming a leadership role, to work above the fray. The ability to step back and view the entire situation is vital because the chaos and tension inherent in a crisis can hinder the interventionist's ability to assess what is transpiring and what needs to be done. It's understandable that school crisis interventionists can become immersed in their duties and pausing to assess the situation might seem to go against the need to intervene quickly. It's advisable, however, that at specific points during the day, and even during the most trying circumstances, the interventionist take a brief break to review what is transpiring and what has transpired. This also helps the interventionist reenergize—emotional and physical fatigue is an important concern during a crises response.

Take in Stride Displays of Hostility and Appreciation

Those who decide to become involved in a crisis intervention effort, whether at the school or district level, no doubt consider their service laudable, and rightly so. However, non-school-based support providers occasionally draw the ire of some within the school population. Though unsettling, it is important to recognize that this is a normal reaction born out of the concern that "outside assistance adds to confusion [and] increases the stress of an already difficult situation," which may result in "feelings of frustration, helplessness, and inadequacy in the school staff" (Heath & Sheen, 2005, p. 3). Conversely, school-based personnel should keep in mind the best efforts of outside assistance, such as mental health or juvenile justice professionals, who are uniquely qualified to render certain services (Schonfeld & Newgass, 2003).

The *Messiah complex* also represents a danger for those serving on crisis intervention teams. Members of the school population might view interventionists as saviors of sorts, people who alone have the ability to lessen the emotional pain that they are experiencing. It's of course wonderful when we can help those in need, but common sense tells us that we don't have the answers to all problems and questions. Humility and honesty with ourselves about our abilities and limitations serves everyone involved during a crisis.

Evaluate and Learn From Mistakes

We'd like to believe that most crisis responses are successful, but interventionists should be able to acknowledge that *mistakes and oversights do occur.* In reflecting on procedures undertaken, a team might resolve that, in the future, the principal will make a more sensitive announcement to the school population over the intercom, or the counselor will instead use solution-focused group therapy techniques, or the school psychologist will show the same level of empathy for grieving staff members as for students. Rarely, if ever, does someone respond to a crisis and not feel that, just maybe, he or she could have done something different to make the intervention more effective.

It's important to remember that school crisis intervention is not an exact science. Working conditions can be tense during these times and mistakes often occur, yet school crisis interventionists should be cautious about overprotecting against mistakes and liability, because this could hinder their effectiveness (Zirkel & Gluckman, 1996). Identifying an error or oversight is a great opportunity to address the mistake and work to remedy it. This learning opportunity can only make for better interventions in future crises.

That being said, at one time or another, we've all been made aware of our mistakes. Some colleagues and superiors can point out these mistakes and we walk away appreciative, having a desire to do better the next time. We value their input and suggestions with no slight whatsoever to our dignity. Unfortunately, others might observe our performance, identify our mistakes, and due to tactlessness, we become defensive or insulted. It hurts! So, colleagues should be approached in a *tactful, sensitive manner* when they make a mistake or oversight during a crisis intervention.

Also, be aware that the nature of crisis-related events can make even the most experienced interventionist sensitive and in no mood for a critique. These interventionists might be more receptive and amenable to suggestions or critique during postcrisis debriefing sessions, and not immediately after the action that needs to be addressed.

Helpful Tips

- If you are a non-school-based crisis interventionist and have been summoned to lend support at another school, be sure to inform office personnel of your destination before you exit your school. This will make it easier for your school to contact you if necessary.
- Predetermine times to take a break, if possible, during a crisis response. These respites can be used to rest and assess the day's activities upto that point. For example, 10:00 and 1:30 are good midmorning and midafternoon times for a brief time out.
- When a colleague's crisis intervention performance necessitates remediation, avoid conducting this activity in an informal setting. Rather, use formal settings such as debriefing sessions and scheduled meetings to address his or her oversights and mistakes.

Questions for Discussion

1. Effective crisis interventionists possess many admirable attributes, such as those listed in this chapter. Are there others that you feel are necessary? Explain the reasons for your response.

2. Have you ever been placed in a position of leadership during a crisis? How did you mobilize your team and delegate responsibility? Were you able work above the fray? If not, why?

3. During a crisis intervention, have you or a colleague ever experienced hostility from students or staff members? What was the reason for that hostility? How did you or your colleague address the situation?

4. Have you ever found it necessary to point out a colleague's mistake or oversight during a crisis intervention? How did that colleague accept it? Do you take criticism well in regard to the provision of crisis intervention?

Training of School Crisis Intervention Team Members

Going to War Without a Weapon?

Jefferson Middle School has regularly been beset by crisis-related events as the result of gang activities occurring near the school. Though many students of this inner-city school have become desensitized to the sights and sounds of the neighborhood violence, it's also quite common for students to require psychological support.

Three weeks prior to the start of the school year, the school's principal is surprised by the unexpected retirement of long-time school counselor Silvia Morales. During Mrs. Morales's 20 years at the school, she has provided invaluable support, especially in the area of working with students during traumatic situations. The principal begins to schedule interviews, but due to the school's poor reputation, draws from a limited list of applicants.

On the final day of interviews, the principal interviews Carrie Ellsworth, a recent graduate from a well-respected West Coast university. After reviewing her resume and application, the principal proceeds to commend Ellsworth based on her academic achievements. He asks about her ability to conduct academic testing, and Ellsworth indicates that she has had coursework in this area. She also indicates that she has had instruction in career counseling, as well as extensive coursework with special populations, including exceptional students. Ellsworth voices her eagerness to secure the job, and adds that she would also like to conduct divorce counseling groups. She even comments, "I would even be willing to check for head lice!"

The principal has saved his most important question for last. With only minutes remaining until the next scheduled interview, he asks Ellsworth about her training with traumatized students in crisis-related situations. After a long pause, Ellsworth informs the principal that though she has had extensive coursework on interventions with various populations, crisis intervention wasn't one of the areas that she had the option of studying. She indicates that she is willing to learn more about school crisis intervention if given the opportunity.

After all remaining interviews have been concluded, Ellsworth is hired. Although her lack of crisis intervention skills is a drawback, her enthusiasm and willingness to learn more about intervention are especially impressive to the principal. On her hiring, the principal informs Ellsworth that she will be required to receive crisis intervention training immediately. He then asks his assistant principal to contact the school district regarding upcoming training options for his new counselor.

Picture yourself in the place of the assistant principal after being asked to arrange for crisis intervention training for the new counselor. Where would you go in your district to find this training? If training is indeed available, is it extensive and effective? Examining these two specific questions begs a much broader question: "Are the majority of school personnel who actually perform crisis intervention adequately trained?"

Fortunately, Ellsworth's principal realized before he hired his new middle school counselor that crisis intervention training was absolutely essential to her ability to serve the school.

WHEN TRAINING IS INADEQUATE

Offering both general and technical crisis intervention training to staff requires planning, time, and the allocation of funds. But when training is lacking, the cost that schools pay in terms of both financial and human resources is unthinkable. Before delving into issues of training, let's first examine how inadequate training can affect the following segments of the school population and community.

Students

Students are the most obvious victims when support personnel are not properly trained to handle a crisis. For instance, in a counseling venue, saying or even indicating the wrong thing to a student can be detrimental to mental and emotional recovery. Proper training also helps crisis intervention team members recognize students whose behaviors are indicative of emotional trauma, regardless of whether these students have sought counseling or support. Missing the opportunity to identify these at-risk students denies them the chance to address difficulties that may have confronted them for a significant period of time.

After a crisis, school personnel might, unintentionally or intentionally, permit students to exit campus, which would allow them to potentially engage in harmful unsupervised activities, such as drinking, driving while in an emotionally unstable state, or engaging in violent behaviors. School personnel must be aware of lockdown procedures and steps for securing their campus. A lack of knowledge regarding "crowd movement" following a crisis can delay or even negate the provision of crisis support services (Chapter 4).

Students can also be negatively affected by inaccurate or insensitive information from school personnel, via announcement or rumor. School administrators should remain fully aware of and sensitive to all information disseminated to the school population.

CRISIS INTERVENTION TEAM MEMBERS

Although we don't usually think of interventionists as the victims of inadequate crisis intervention training, they can be. When an interventionist responds to a crisis, it is frequently under very stressful or tense conditions. Compound this fact with the reality that some of these support providers did not receive adequate training, and one can easily see how interventionists can become overwhelmed. Addressing the needs of a traumatized school population is enormously challenging and it's virtually impossible to fake competency when engaged in the provision of crisis intervention services. Interventionists who don't possess the skills necessary to render effective support can understandably become emotionally or physically fatigued or will occasionally choose to remove themselves from crisis response responsibilities. Consequently, the school or its district might unnecessarily lose an interventionist who might have provided years of effective services had training been originally offered.

Other Staff Members

One of many crisis intervention tasks is consultation with staff members, including administrators, teachers, and non-instructional staff (Allen, Burt, et al., 2002). Consultation remains an important task that should be provided only by trained interventionists. The provision of consultation by untrained interventionists presents significant difficulties because erroneous information or ill-advised recommendations can quickly or inaccurately be communicated to large numbers of students via the staff member.

Crisis counseling in the hands of untrained interventionists remains a precarious endeavor as they interact with students, but it is also a concern as interventionists attempt to address the needs of staff members during counseling interventions as well.

The School and the Community's Reputation

Schools are a direct reflection of the community in which they are located. The manner in which schools deal with crises often becomes widely known throughout the community. This is often seen in newspaper articles that depict the manner in which a school population came together after a tragedy or, conversely, experienced difficulty rebounding from a tragedy. In either case, crisis interventionists remain at the center of the school's ability to recover following a traumatic event, and they remain instrumental in whether a school gains a good or poor reputation for its resilience and ability to provide for its students and staff during difficult times.

HOW ARE SCHOOL CRISIS INTERVENTIONISTS PREPARED?

Now that we've established that school crisis interventionists should receive thorough training and that the ramifications of inadequate training are serious, the next critical question is, "Who is actually responsible for the provision of crisis intervention training?" Training is typically offered at first in preservice education as part of the coursework required to earn a graduate degree. School districts then provide subsequent (and ideally ongoing) training to staff members. Occasionally school staffs feel undertrained with regard to crisis intervention. Though school systems are mainly responsible for preparing their staffs to respond during a crisis, many districts differ in the degree to which the responsibility of crisis intervention training is prioritized. As a result, interventionists in one district might be exceptionally well prepared to render supportive services, whereas personnel in other districts remain ill prepared to provide school crisis intervention services.

PRESERVICE TRAINING

I recognize that readers of this book are primarily practicing educators who cannot control crisis intervention training that occurs at the graduate level. Nonetheless, this section presents statistics on preservice education with regard to crisis intervention to further underscore the need for training in the school system.

Personnel who typically assume the responsibility of providing crisis intervention support have usually attained one or more graduate level degrees. These support providers include guidance counselors, school social workers, school nurses, and school psychologists. It is assumed that graduate programs provide crisis intervention coursework, but how effective is that training? Melissa Allen, together with two different teams of researchers from Brigham Young University (Allen, Burt, et al., 2002; Allen, Jerome, et al., 2002), conducted studies of the preservice preparation of both school counselors and school psychologists.

Training of School Counselors

Allen, Burt, et al. (2002) asked 276 school counselors to indicate the extent to which they felt their university coursework had prepared them to engage in crisis intervention activities on a scale of 1 (not at all prepared) to 5 (very well prepared). The results revealed that the counselors felt "less than adequately prepared" to handle a crisis situation ($M = 2.52$, $SD = 1.06$). The percentage of the counselors who reported feeling "minimally prepared" or "not prepared at all" to handle crisis situations was 57%. Although 24% of the school counselors revealed that they were "adequately prepared," only 18% of the total sample indicated that their university coursework helped them to feel "well prepared or "very well prepared" to handle a school crisis.

Training of School Psychologists

Allen, Jerome, et al. (2002) surveyed 276 school psychologists regarding their university training in relation to crisis intervention. Of the school psychologists, 58% reported that they felt they were minimally prepared or not prepared at all to handle school crises. Only 2% of the school psychologists indicated that they were well prepared or very well prepared to address a school crisis. On the whole, school psychologists felt that they would have liked additional university training, particularly in the areas of suicide, aggression and violence, and school district crisis plans (Allen, Jerome, White, Pope, & Malinka, 2001).

One way that practitioners can affect university crisis intervention training is by providing feedback to schools of education and nursing on the skills that can be taught through coursework. In addition, many practitioners seek higher education degrees through night school. This affords them the opportunity to directly apply learning in the school setting. Practitioners who are also enrolled in education programs have direct access to academics and may be able to influence future course offerings and their content, as well as practicums and internship experiences, based on sharing school needs. (Allen, Burt, et al., 2002)

Adelman (Adleman, 1996; Adelman & Taylor, 2006) explains that in order to improve crisis intervention skills, practice and supervision must be provided for graduate students. In order to provide more opportunities in crisis intervention during practicums and internships, they go on to emphasize the need for school districts and community agencies to coordinate crisis intervention approaches and activities.

INSERVICE PROFESSIONAL DEVELOPMENT

Professional development remains a major component in the preparation of crisis interventionists. Schonfeld and Newgass (2003) assert that, "Given proper training, support, and resources, school staff are well situated to provide children and adolescents with triage, support, services, short-term counseling, and referral to community services during and after a crisis" (p. 1). Of course, "proper training" is a key factor in the success of any intervention effort. And though it's important for teachers, counselors, psychologists, nurses, and others in school to "actively seek and participate in professional development activities that increase the knowledge and skills in the area of crisis intervention" (p. 100), the decision to design and offer training rests with the district-level crisis intervention team. District-level intervention teams do much more than oversee the implementation of school-based crisis intervention plans and occasionally swoop into schools when disaster strikes. Schonfeld and Newgass (2003) have identified that a core responsibility of the district-level team is that it "requires and arranges training of school-based crisis intervention teams" (p. 3). In the Allen, Jerome, et al. (2002) survey of school psychologists, 75% reported that school districts provided opportunities or financial assistance for their training. Approximately 81% of the school psychologists reported that their training was at the local level, including inservices provided by the school district, local speakers, and seminars within the community. About 64% of the school psychologists indicated that they also secured crisis intervention information via books, journal articles, and or materials published by the National Association of School Psychologists (NASP).

If leadership from the district is lacking, school administrators are in a position to petition the district for the development of a training program or allocate local funds to provide the much-needed professional development. Feedback from practitioners is invaluable in directing research efforts and deciding on the most pertinent topics to cover in crisis intervention training.

TIPS FOR TRAINING INADEQUATELY PREPARED SCHOOL CRISIS INTERVENTION TEAMS

1. Once an inadequate or untrained school crisis intervention team has been identified, the decision to secure training

should be made immediately. The longer an inadequately prepared team is allowed to provide services, the greater the chances of oversights that will negatively affect the school population.

2. Assess individuals who will be included in crisis intervention response regarding their degree of crisis intervention experience. For instance, one would assess their knowledge of counseling skills, logistical response, interaction with media personnel, and level of comfort in intense situations.

3. Decide if all crisis support personnel will participate in training, or if beginner and advanced trainings will be made available. If a crisis interventionist has performed his or her duties for a significant length of time, and as a result is reluctant to participate in a training that he or she feels is better left to newer team members, the administrator or crisis team leader can simply inform the seasoned interventionist that the training is a refresher course of sorts. Every member of a crisis response team should be on the same page regarding the provision of his or her intervention efforts, even if it means retraining or providing a review for all team members in an effort to raise the overall performance of that team.

All crisis intervention team members are advised to undergo *general* training. This training should cover the following aspects, as identified by the Center for Mental Health in Schools at UCLA (2005, p. 51):

- How to minimize student spread of negative ideas or emotions after the crisis event occurs
- How to reassure the majority of students about what has taken place
- How to determine who will need psychological first aid and how to provide it to those most in need (including those in shock or clearly experiencing trauma)
- How to apply appropriate counseling skills (such as active listening, small-group counseling techniques, conflict resolution, critical incident stress debriefing, and support group facilitation)

Specialized training, then, offers instruction in skills "with respect to a specific type of crisis" such as fire, earthquake, suicide, and so on. This training would cover the "types of reactions students, staff, and parents are likely to have to a particular type of crisis, and how to respond to specific types of reactions" (Center for Mental Health in Schools at UCLA, 2005, p. 51).

4. If some members of the school crisis intervention team haven't received adequate training through a university or school system, determine who will provide future training. Are there individuals on the team who can provide the training or is it necessary to look to the district-level team or a community agency?

5. After the "beginner" school crisis interventionist has received training, allow him or her to be observed or shadowed by an experienced interventionist in crisis event simulations. This consultation ensures that oversights, mistakes, or effective interventions can be identified.

6. Once the original trainings have been offered, determine how often refresher trainings will be made available for the crisis interventionists. Will the refreshers be offered after each semester, biannually, yearly? It's also a good idea to schedule regular meetings to allow team members to discuss how they reacted during previous call outs or events, and to address any need or problem that emerged from these events. Team meetings are also an opportune times to disseminate information regarding crisis response via guest speaker, inservice activity, or the review of current and relevant research. In addition, new crisis team members can be introduced, and existing or altered procedure discussed.

EVALUATING THE EFFECTIVENESS OF THE TRAINING

In discussing his school's crisis intervention response team, a middle school administrator asked, "Now that they've been trained, how do I know if my school's crisis response team is actually effective?" This was a very important question because during a crisis, the assessment of interventionists who have been trained and are providing services is generally overlooked. How have they actually performed? Were they effective? As we have seen, an incompetent crisis interventionist can be the source of many unnecessary problems. Neglecting the assessment of these interventionists allows their work, however ineffective or deficient, to continue as they become involved in future crises responses. Conversely, to remediate the work of this same interventionist is to benefit the members of the school population who are reacting to a crisis and seeking support.

Unfortunately, methods for objectively rating crisis intervention performance are rare and for the most part not implemented by many school districts. Evaluations of crisis intervention efforts traditionally occur informally during debriefing sessions scheduled immediately following the crisis or several days after the crisis. The administrator or crisis team leader does, however, have the option of taking preventive measures to ensure that his or her charges follow appropriate steps, perform necessary techniques, implement counseling formats, and address or avoid crisis-related topics. It should be emphasized that this initial crisis intervention training option should be made available to everyone on a crisis response team who is in the position to provide crisis intervention support, not to only a select few.

The specific delivery of psychological support and accountability during crisis intervention should never be taken lightly. Interventionists must keep in mind that students or staff members who seek psychological assistance may be vulnerable to further emotional distress if the interventionist is unprepared or not cognizant of adequate crisis intervention techniques, formats, or approaches. Unprepared interventionists only invite traumatized individuals to experience further emotional difficulty that may otherwise have been avoided if proper training procedures had been available. Preparation is the key to success, and never is this more evident than as it relates to the provision of psychological support during a school crisis.

Helpful Tips

- Be proactive! If you feel that your school or district's crisis intervention training opportunities are inadequate, don't hesitate to contact district and/or local university personnel in an effort to secure sufficient training.
- Be on the lookout for school crisis intervention trainings and inservices offered within your district, at conferences, your community, or at local universities.
- Personnel within universities, local mental health centers, or out-of-district presenters often offer their services as outside consultants for school personnel who serve on school crisis intervention teams. Be on the lookout!

Questions for Discussion

1. How did you receive your training in school crisis intervention? Was your instruction provided at the school district level or university level? Was any of this training secured on your own through reading journals or by attending conferences and workshops?

2. Have you ever observed a colleague attempt to engage a student and it became obvious that he or she lacked adequate crisis intervention training? What was your reaction? To the best of your knowledge, was this colleague ever the recipient of adequate training? If not, why?

3. Does your school district provide adequate crisis intervention training? If not, what can be done to remedy this problem? With whom could you discuss this critical issue?

ISSUE FOUR

Logistical School Crisis Response

The Overlooked Intervention

Prior to the start of the school year, the Millvale school board proudly announce the formation of a district crisis intervention team. This 15-member, non-school-based team is composed of social workers, psychologists, and nurses. During the summer and end of the previous school year, the team underwent training that heavily emphasized mental health support for the district's 29 schools in the event they were confronted with crisis-related situations.

Two weeks after the school board's introduction of the team, the unit's supervisor is notified that two basketball players have been killed in a car accident after their Thursday night game. The victims were both highly visible and popular seniors, and as a result, the entire crisis team is summoned to Allen Senior High School. Upon arrival, the team members find a chaotic situation in which approximately 200 students have converged on the media center where guidance personnel have gathered and attempted to provide support. Other school personnel are observed frantically attempting to steer students

41

into other rooms or areas where support can be rendered. Many students are seen running toward the parking lot in an effort to leave campus to visit the crash site.

On her arrival, the crisis team chair, Karen Miller, locates the principal and introduces herself. She asks for plans or recommendations but the administrator pleads, "Please, just get my school under control. I've never seen anything like this. It's total mayhem out there and we just aren't prepared!"

Outside of the media center, Miller notices about 50 students milling about, consoling each other. Inside, she finds many students sobbing uncontrollably, walking about with little supervision. Miller notices eight of her crisis unit members attempting to seat students in an effort to start counseling sessions. The remaining seven team members are either in the school hallways or the guidance suite, also attempting to direct the onslaught of students to their appropriate counseling areas. Adding to the confusion is the fact that counseling venues have not previously been identified.

Prior to noon, little has been done in the way of counseling intervention because most efforts have been directed toward crowd control. The afternoon also sees little in the way of psychological support intervention. Although the team and school staff appear exhausted, Miller reminds her team and the school-based crisis support providers that a debriefing will be conducted immediately after dismissal in the principal's conference room.

As the debriefing begins, Miller detects frustration, especially among her team members. She identifies the main source of the frustration as the team's inability to provide mental health support in lieu of its chief duty, which on this day was crowd control. One team member emotionally opines that the team's intense training has been of little use, because the main intervention had very little to do with counseling and mental health support. He states, "We didn't get to do our thing. I felt like a babysitter—a traffic cop out there!"

What happened at Allen Senior High School? Was the school prepared for the news of the tragedy? Was the district's crisis team prepared? It's obvious that neither school personnel nor the crisis team was ready for the influx of students that sought support. The crisis team did, however, learn a very valuable lesson that so many schools learn: that there are two types of crisis responses; the first response deals with the physical movement of students or staff as a result of a crisis and the school's reaction to this movement. I call this *logistical crisis response*. It is a critical aspect of crisis intervention but unfortunately is often overlooked. The second type of crisis intervention deals with the provision of *psychological support* or "psychological first aid" (Pynoos & Nader, 1988). This is the type of involvement most people think of when school crisis intervention is mentioned and usually consists of counseling or the provision of mental health support for distraught students and staff. It's imperative to realize that the absence of preplanned logistical intervention can prevent even the most competent crisis interventionists from providing psychological support. Simply put, you can't provide emotional or psychological support for individuals who aren't there. An effective logistical plan can ensure that students and staff members are available for the support they need.

ORGANIZED RESPONSE IS THE DIFFERENCE BETWEEN SUCCESS AND FAILURE

The difference between a smooth crisis response and a disorganized one lies in the manner in which the affected student population was managed immediately after they were made aware of the situation. I've observed events that should have been addressed by interventionists with little or no difficulty unexpectedly explode into chaos. Conversely, I've witnessed events that I could almost have guaranteed would be problematic, only to have the school population minimally disturbed. In both instances, it was the manner in which the student population was managed after learning of the crisis that made the difference.

Logistical crisis response requires forethought and the establishment of a plan prior to a "crisis." The worst possible time to consider a logistical plan is during the actual crisis, but unfortunately this is when schools often become aware of its importance. Ironically, the absence of a preplanned logistical response usually occurs only once, as the unprepared school becomes immediately aware of its necessity as a prerequisite for effective crisis response. It's wise to avoid this dilemma in the first place.

What occurred at Allen Senior High School could have been avoided if a simple preplanned logistical response was established. However, it served as a dramatic example of how a school (or district) can on one hand be prepared for the inevitable in the area of mental health support but on the other hand be at a loss as to methods for getting mental health support initiated.

Logistical tasks must be clearly identified and delineated if schools are to create the conditions that allow for the delivery of mental and psychological support. As Schonfeld and Newgass (2003) assert, "Schools are better able to function with minimal disruption in the aftermath of a crisis if they have sufficient structure in place to coordinate services when the crisis occurs" (p. 5). Logistical duties might include the following roles and functions, as identified by the Center for Mental Health in Schools at UCLA (2005):

- Mobilizing the team when needed (e.g., telephone trees)
- Coordinating communications and controlling rumors
- Handling crowd management
- Contacting the media and answering questions
- Organizing evacuation and transportation (p. 10)

Once these roles have been determined and the logistical plan drawn up, the plan must be used and reviewed regularly to ensure that that all staff are familiar with it. Once implemented, the plan should be reviewed at regular intervals for revisions and improvements.

DEVELOPING A LOGISTICAL PLAN OF ACTION

Like any other plan of action within a school, there are necessary steps regarding the establishment of a logistical crisis response. Five important steps include determining the answers to these questions:

1. When is the best time for a school to establish a logistical response plan?

2. Which staff members should be involved in logistical crisis response?

3. How should staff members be activated during a crisis?

4. Where will counseling and support venues be located and how will sessions be administered?

5. Should students be allowed to exit the campus after a crisis?

All of these questions should be addressed before the vital logistical response plan can be established for a school campus. First, however, it's important to acknowledge that any school crisis response team should distinguish between those staff members who will address crowd control (logistical interventionist) and those who will provide some form of counseling (mental health/psychological interventionists). Non-school-based crisis teams or interventionists are better left to the provision of mental health support because they might understandably lack an awareness of counseling venues or the overall knowledge of the physical lay out of a campus. That's not to say, however, that certain school-based staff members shouldn't be involved in the provision of mental health support. For example, a health teacher or psychology teacher might be permitted to conduct mental health counseling if he or she has adequate training. The team leader should assign both logistical and mental health roles prior to a crisis occurring.

When Is the Best Time for a School to Establish a Logistical Response Plan?

The best time for an administrator to establish a logistical crisis response plan is prior to the beginning of the school year, preferably during preplanning sessions. This provides a safeguard a crisis in case occurs early in the school year, and, in addition, staff energy and enthusiasm are usually high as the school year begins. Keep in mind, that the most *inopportune* time to establish a plan is after a crisis has occurred.

When the staff meeting is held to discuss this issue, it should be the sole item on the agenda, which will serve to underscore its importance. Also, the administrator should mandate that every staff manner attend the meeting, including paraprofessionals and noninstructional staff members. At no time should a staff member be excused in order to address other school-related matters, because no circumstance takes precedence over crisis intervention.

Procedures and assignments should be posted on a blackboard, chart, or overhead. A designated meeting secretary should record ideas discussed and roles assigned. Following the meeting, a packet containing the relevant information produced during the meeting should be distributed to staff.

During this meeting, the principal could also identify the interventionists who will provide the psychological support during a crisis. These staff members usually include guidance counselors, school social workers, nurses, school psychologists, human relation specialists, or any other faculty trained in the provision of mental health support. In addition, if a district crisis team is available, its role should be discussed during this meeting.

Which Staff Members Should Be Involved In Logistical Crisis Response?

Each staff member, in some way, could conceivably be involved in the provision of logistical crisis response. From the start of the faculty meeting, the principal or other designee should repeatedly emphasize that logistical crisis response is everyone's responsibility, and, if necessary, all staff should be expected to assist. In an effort to reduce the anxiety of those suspicious or wary of crisis intervention efforts, the principal should also point out that logistical crisis response will not involve counseling or any other task for which members of the staff have not received training. The clear identification of pertinent logistical roles is a necessity for school administrators.

The following roles could be assumed by school personnel in lieu of providing psychological support during a school crisis:

> *School resource officers*—Maintaining order on campus, directing student traffic, securing the campus, and gathering information
>
> *Teachers*—Maintaining order in their classrooms, monitoring hallways, directing student traffic, providing student information to school crisis interventionists
>
> *School nurses*—Providing medical support, consulting with school personnel, directing student traffic
>
> *School administrators*—Coordinating crisis response efforts, media contacts, consulting with school personnel and crisis team members, directing student traffic, meeting with parents
>
> *Noninstructional support personnel*—Providing logistical support, assisting with school considerations such as room arrangements, refreshments, and tissues. (Basham, Appleton, & Dykeman, 2000)

Regardless of who participates in the crisis response, it's important for schools and districts to rotate members, if possible. This rotation prevents interventionists from becoming emotionally or physically fatigued as the result of excessive crisis assignments or call outs. It also allows other, possibly less-experienced, team members to benefit from exposure to crises.

On occasion, a school will become well acquainted and comfortable with a specific interventionist and desire or even insist on that person's services during any crisis-related event(s). Though the interventionist might also feel comfortable and actually welcome these future requests, it is wise for crisis team administrators to monitor or even limit "requests" for a particular interventionist in order to guard against fatigue.

How Should Staff Members Be Activated During a Crisis?

Many schools use a code or slogan over PA announcements that indicates to staff when a situation has or is about to transpire. For example, a principal desiring to lock down a campus due to the presence of an intruder might interrupt class to make an announcement as simple as, "code purple" or use a coded phrase such as, "There will be sandwiches available for the faculty in the cafeteria after school." Either announcement could indicate that a lockdown is in progress. Likewise, when a crisis occurs, a simple phrase can alert faculty that they should prepare to activate for a logistical crisis response. (Of course, their duties will have been assigned before the announcement). After this phrase or code is relayed to the faculty, the administrator can proceed to make an announcement to the general student population. After the announcement has been made, if a large number of frenzied students move throughout the school or converge on a specific area, designated interventionists will be prepared to intercept these students and direct them to areas where support will be available.

The Timing, Nature, and Manner of Announcements

One of the most (if not *the* most) difficult tasks that a school administrator will be called on to perform is informing his or her school population of a tragedy. Announcements are critical since they can set a tone that will ultimately dictate how a school population reacts. Announcements should be made with three critical considerations in mind:

1. The *timing* of the announcement

2. The *content* of the announcement

3. The *manner* in which the announcement is made

Timing. When should a school administrator make an announcement about a tragedy? This is a difficult but extremely important question. The longer the announcement is delayed during the school day, the more the opportunity for rumors increases, which might lead to more difficulty for crisis interventionists, faculty, and school administration. *Announcements should be made early in the school day, if possible.* This allows crisis intervention team members ample opportunity to provide support for the affected school population, as well as to prevent rumors from spreading throughout the campus. Announcements should be made only when the facts of the situation are known. Predictions and small details regarding the situation should be avoided.

Content. Administrators often ask, "How much detail should we provide?" Basic information is acceptable. However, over-saturating the school with detail only leads to further difficulties because the information can be misconstrued by members of the school population. The administrator might attempt to focus on feelings in an effort to interrupt the school population's desire for details. For example, if accurate information is unavailable, an appropriate administrative response might be, "At this time, details of Joseph's condition are unknown; however, we are all concerned. Please keep him in your thoughts. We will announce any further information when it becomes available during the course of the school day."

Manner. The manner in which an announcement is made is also critical. If a school population perceives the administrator to be "matter of fact" or unsympathetic during the announcement, an angry reaction could result. This, unfortunately, compounds the task of crisis interventionists because this anger must be diffused prior to the provision of support (Jaksec, 2001).

Where Will Counseling and Support Venues Be Located and How Will Sessions Be Administered?

When schools scramble to find locations to render support to students or staff, it is a sure sign of poor logistical crisis intervention planning. Organization is a prerequisite for logistical intervention, and something as simple as predesignating areas or venues for crisis support services can prevent chaos and undue disorganization (Jaksec, 2001).

This is especially evident in secondary school settings when students who are reacting to the crisis make their way into hallways, wander around the campus, or converge on support areas such as guidance suites, media centers, or auditoriums. Crises that confront elementary schools rarely pose these logistical difficulties because younger students are more easily contained. They are usually too frightened to leave the classroom; subsequently crisis interventionists can proceed to their classrooms.

A small amount of preplanning can easily prevent chaotic situations, which occur more frequently when adequate logistical plans have not been established. When establishing a logistical crisis response plan, designate *several* venues for the provision of future crisis intervention services. It's impossible to predict the number of students and staff that will need future interventions, but a school can usually identify enough venues to effectively handle a significant portion of its population as it reacts to a crisis.

During an event that affects a small portion of the school population, a logical place to render crisis services could be a room that can comfortably hold eight to ten students. In addition, several other medium-sized rooms should be identified; they might include counseling and psychological support offices, principal's conference rooms, or even unused classrooms. During a large-scale crisis affecting a large portion of the school population, media centers, auditoriums, or gymnasiums might be designated. All smaller venues should be utilized before larger venues are considered.

Naturally, when leading a group counseling session, different leaders will be comfortable with different group sizes. If done outside of the classroom, facilitators may feel comfortable with groups ranging from 7 to 12 individuals. Brock (Brock, Lazarus, & Jimerson, 2002) explains that crisis intervention groups are most effective with sizes ranging from 15 to 30 students. Young (2002, as cited in Brock, et al., 2002) recommends 20 to 25 individuals in group interventions. Large groups can restrict group sharing and limit the expression of feelings (Schonfeld, 1989, as cited in Brock, et al., 2002). Groups in excess of 40 individuals are not recommended (Bell, 1995, and Mitchell & Everly, 1996, as cited in Brock, et al., 2002). Have a plan in place for crises of varying scope so that enough groups can be formed to facilitate effective support sessions. The reality, of course, may be that on-site personnel are limited and so larger groups are the only option. Another factor that might determine the size of a group counseling session is the emotional makeup of the students and staff who seek to participate in the counseling session. If students or staff are highly emotionally charged due to the situation, facilitating a group with a larger number of participants might be more difficult than facilitating a smaller, more manageable group.

I recommend that group sessions not exceed ten students if possible. It's imperative that after the session has begun, no other individuals be allowed to enter the group. (Special exceptions can be made at the group facilitator's discretion.) This interruption interferes with the rhythm that the facilitator seeks to establish in the counseling session. One simple way of preventing the inclusion of additional group members is by taping a sign on the door stating, "SESSION CLOSED" and also adding additional information that states when and where the next session will take place. It is important that students who are turned away due to group size restrictions know that their needs will be addressed.

When a frazzled crisis interventionist experiences difficulty controlling the behavior of the individuals in the group session, this difficulty can often stem from the fact that no

rules for behavior were established before the session com-
menced. It should be emphasized that establishing rules prior
to group counseling is imperative and results in a more effective and orderly group session.

If the establishment of rules does not take place, students
invariably engage in intentional or unintentional behaviors that
can quickly sabotage a counseling session. As simple and implied
as some of the following rules seem, they nonetheless should be
discussed and agreed on before a group counseling session com-
mences. According to Brock (Brock, et al. 2002), allowing students
to assist with group rules helps to establish an environment
in which students are seen as capable problem solvers. Rules
should cover respectful behavior to oneself and others, the
degree to which physical contact with others will be allowed during the session, and when students will be allowed to leave the
session. This book includes common questions and answers to
help those involved in group counseling facilitation ensure that
respectful behavior takes place once a session is initiated.

Should Students Be Allowed to Exit Campus After a Crisis?

The answer to this question depends on the various
factors that the planning group must weigh, and of course the
severity of the crisis. Schonfeld and Newgass (2003) advise
that schools should continue with routine activities, if possible, and avoid letting students leave campus early. The reasons for this are numerous:

> Students find comfort in the school day routine and in the
> company of their peers and trusted adults. In addition,
> canceling school disrupts the family routine and places
> an additional burden on working parents who must
> scramble to find alternate childcare. . . . Further, temporary
> removal from school can sometimes increase a student's
> fears about returning to school and may engender school
> avoidance behaviors. (p. 5)

In some instances, a student might benefit from being removed from campus. For example, when a student threatens violence in response to the crisis and necessitates the involvement of legal authorities, or due to his or her emotional instability, a student requires more intense mental health support from a private or community-based agency.

Helpful Tips

- Ensure that critical crisis intervention roles are assigned to staff who are on-site full time, in addition to non-school-based crisis teams that will be on-site shortly. This ensures that the majority of staff can respond immediately to the situation at hand.
- Use *simple* codes or verbal announcements when indicating crisis situations. Also, periodically review the code throughout the school year.
- Predesignate counseling venues that will accommodate various size counseling groups.
- Team leaders should provide packets to all crisis interventionists with pertinent information regarding duties and procedures.

Questions for Discussion

1. Do you think your school could currently address the movement of a multitude of students as the result of a traumatic event? Does your school have a logistical crisis response plan? If so, has it proven to be effective?

2. Sketch a logistical response plan for your school. For instance, how would the staff be notified of a crisis? Who would be in charge of student movement? What locations would you assign as support venues? Could logistical problems arise that are specific to your school?

3. Have you ever been involved in the provision of crisis intervention when an effective logistical response plan had not been established? If so, how did this affect the school's overall ability to address the needs of its students and staff?

Determining the Impact of a Crisis

How Big Will the Bang Be?

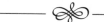

At 11:30 on a Thursday night, Sally Miller, assistant principal of Tanner Middle School, is awakened by a telephone call from a frantic colleague. As she attempts to clear her head, she asks her longtime coworker what has happened. The teacher explains that she learned that the school's principal died suddenly two hours earlier at a local restaurant. Miller hangs up the phone, struggling to absorb the news. Overcome with emotion, Miller refuses to believe that her mentor has died. While her husband attempts to provide comfort, Miller realizes that she is now, for all intents and purposes, the head administrator at a middle school with more than 1,300 students. Even in her distress, Miller's first consideration is the impact that her principal's death will have on the large student population. The 52-year-old principal, who had served the school in various capacities for 15 years, was highly visible on campus and popular with both students and staff members.

Throughout the night, Miller receives numerous calls from personnel within her school district. One call from the supervisor of the district's crisis intervention team offers support and the promise that the crisis team will be available for the school during the following days. The supervisor asks Miller to predict the impact that the news of the death will have on the students and staff. Miller responds that the impact will, of course, be enormous. The supervisor persists and asks Miller to try to be specific since Tanner Middle School's population has been shaken by the loss of two teachers and the critical injury of a popular student in the past two years.

The main purpose for asking this question is actually to assess the number of responders necessary and the response strategies to be implemented by the district crisis intervention team and school-based support personnel. Miller informs the district team supervisor that, unfortunately, the school has no active crisis intervention team. She also has doubts regarding her staff's ability to handle the situation, especially in light of the popularity of the principal. Tactfully, the supervisor explains to the shaken assistant principal that several variables would factor into the manner in which the school population would respond to the news of the principal's death. For the next half hour, Miller tries to provide the crisis team administrator with information that will prove invaluable regarding the degree and manner in which Tanner Middle School would receive crisis intervention support during the next several days.

Splat! If you filled ten different-sized balloons with water and dropped them on a sidewalk, each of the water "outlines" would differ. When dropped, balloons with a larger capacity would leave a larger water mark on the sidewalk than a smaller balloon with a smaller capacity. In addition, each balloon might produce a different water mark depending on several other factors, including the speed of the balloon when dropped on the sidewalk, the thickness of the balloon, or the surface of the sidewalk. Clearly, the balloon's water mark would be determined by several factors.

Similarly, when a school faces a crisis situation, the impact of the event will invariably be determined by several factors that schools must take into consideration before intervention is initiated. However, anyone who has ever engaged in school crisis intervention will, in all likelihood, agree that no two crises are alike. It's virtually impossible to gauge exactly how schools will respond when the unfortunate event occurs. I've been summoned to schools and presumed that there would be a minimal need for crisis intervention on the part of the school population, only to be surprised by the number of students and staff who sought assistance. On the other hand, I've also witnessed the loss of highly visible school personnel or students, expecting a large request for services, only to be surprised by the lack of response by the school population.

LOOKING BEFORE YOU LEAP

When a situation emerges that affects a portion or all of the school population, the support provider's goal is to return the campus to normal as soon as possible. This is the immediate goal of crisis intervention—the renormalization of the campus (Schonfeld, Kline, & Members of the Crisis Intervention Committee, 2005). The response, however, must always be coupled with a thorough understanding of several factors that will ultimately dictate the effectiveness and quality of the intervention. By failing to take important variables into consideration prior to intervention, school personnel might blindly enter a turbulent situation that might have been much more effectively addressed if these factors were previously considered.

Determining the level or intensity of a school population's response to a crisis is not an exact science. That being said, on the majority of crisis calls to which I have responded, I've found that a preassessment of the event and close attention to several important variables genuinely benefited the support providers, and ultimately the school population, as they struggled to recover from the situation. First, impact variables should be explored. These factors help determine the degree of reaction by the school population. By attempting to gauge a level of reaction, crisis team leaders can more thoroughly address crucial questions related to response strategy.

ASSESSING IMPACT VARIABLES

Terr (1991, as cited in Basham, Appleton, & Dykeman, 2000) makes a distinction between two types of trauma, Type I and Type II. Type I traumas include unexpected traumatic events such as death, illness, violence, and man-made or natural disasters. The victims remain responsive to counseling and personality changes are not expected, although posttraumatic stress disorders can result as a result of a severe crisis.

Trauma resulting from expected prolonged or anticipated threat or pain is called Type II trauma. Examples of Type II trauma include poverty, war, abuse, and environmental violence. Individuals experiencing chronic trauma require highly specialized and professional intervention. Terr explains that it is essential to distinguish between the types of trauma that students and school personnel may be experiencing as a result of the crisis. Upon determination of these types of trauma, referrals for further support can be made.

Prior to activating team members, crisis team leaders should consider the following questions that might help these leaders make a more accurate prediction of the level of reaction by the school population.

- What type of crisis has befallen the campus?
- When were the most recent crises on this campus?
- Has the school endured frequent crises?
- Does the school have available support staff to effectively handle the crisis?
- When and where did the crisis occur?
- Was the crisis was expected?
- Who was actually affected by the event?

DETERMINING THE SCOPE OF THE CRISIS

The type or magnitude of an event will likely dictate the level of reaction from a school population. Tragedies that received national attention, such as Hurricane Katrina, the *Challenger* space shuttle disaster, and the events of September 11, 2001, were non-school-based, but nonetheless dramatically affected the majority of our nation's school populations. The enormity of these specific events held dramatic meaning for students and faculties. As a result, most school crisis interventionists easily gauged that the events would intensely affect their school populations and adjusted intervention approaches. In contrast to these events are the numerous tragedies that fail to produce the type of response seen in a major national disaster.

At the school level, the death of a little-known student who has succumbed to a long battle with a terminal illness might result in less overall impact on the school population than that of a popular athlete who is killed on his way home from school. Volatile situations such as homicides, suicides, and kidnappings obviously tend to provoke a more emotional response from the school's population. Logically, the larger the magnitude of the crisis, and the greater the emotional attachment to the victim(s), the more intense the reaction of the school population. Support providers should remain cognizant of the type of crisis confronting a school population before engaging those in need, because their crisis intervention approaches might be predicated on the type and intensity of the event. A matrix has been established by the Center for Mental Health in Schools at UCLA (2005) that can assist crisis interventionists in determining the scope of crisis events (see http://smhp.psych.ucla.edu, "Planning for a Crisis," p. 8).

AWARENESS OF THE NUMBER OF CRISES A SCHOOL HAS SUFFERED

Often, the response of a school will be determined by how frequently a particular type of crisis is experienced, and how recently it occurred. If a school has had the misfortune of experiencing a high number of crisis-related events in a short time span, the school will either benefit from regularly addressing the needs of its population during that time, or conversely become fatigued due to the frequency of the crises. I have observed schools react in both directions. Occasionally, a school will experience multiple crisis-related events in a short span and experience a "black cloud" mentality that can pervade the campus atmosphere. "Why us? Why our school?" Unfortunately, few acceptable answers can be provided.

Crisis interventionists should never hesitate to ask school personnel (e.g., administrators, counselors, crisis team leaders), "When was the last time this school was affected by a crisis?" and, "How many crises has this school endured in the past months/years?" These two important questions can shed much light on the school's ability to handle (or not handle) the current situation. In addition, the interventionist might explore how the school has actually reacted to turbulent situations in the past.

AVAILABILITY OF SUPPORT STAFF

One of the primary factors regarding a school's ability to respond to a crisis is the availability of support staff that can be readily accessed when necessary. School districts differ in their approaches to crisis response. Some school districts have established school-based crisis teams and, in addition, have the option of summoning a district-level crisis intervention team if necessary. Other districts have very little in the way of school-based or district-level support during times of crisis.

Prior to a crisis response, support personnel should establish the number of support providers available at the school at that time. This ensures that if adequate support personnel are not available on campus, additional interventionists can be summoned rather than attempting to summon them when the school day is in progress.

As a means to avoid this situation, school-based administrators should make crisis intervention assignments at the beginning of the school year as discussed in Chapter 1.

LOCATION AND TIME OF THE CRISIS

The actual proximity of the crisis to the school can also dramatically affect the degree to which the school population reacts. (We've established, however, that national tragedies can occur thousands of miles away from the school and still have a great impact.) A crisis that occurs on campus might affect students more intensely than a crisis that occurs off campus. This was seen in the vivid footage of students being led out of the Columbine High School campus. On-campus violence could traumatize an entire school population, whereas the same violence, if occurring off campus, might result in a much less dramatic response from the school population.

For the crisis interventionist, knowledge of the proximity of the crisis might dictate the actual intervention approach and techniques that will need to be rendered. For instance, the aforementioned example of on-campus violence might necessitate that the school crisis interventionist initially provide a more logistically oriented service than a phychologically oriented crisis intervention, which can be rendered at a later time.

The actual time of the crisis can also influence the degree of impact on the school population. For example, a car accident occurring on a Friday evening might prevent school personnel from providing support until Monday morning. (This is not to say that other support measures couldn't be secured during the weekend.) On the other hand, if a crisis occurs prior to school or during school time, the impact could be greater. When a tragedy occurs during a weekend or vacation period, school support personnel have the advantage of having more time to plan for the school population's return to campus. It's conceivable that the intensity of reaction to a crisis might decrease if the school population is off campus.

THE IMMEDIACY OF THE CRISIS

Was the crisis expected? How quickly was the school population informed of the news of the crisis? The expected death of a student who had battled a long illness might have a lesser impact on the student population than the sudden suicide of a popular student government officer. The opportunity to brace for a crisis situation might result in the school population being less impacted by the event. Yet the unexpected news of a tragedy can also unfortunately result in a myriad of difficulties, including emotionally charged students moving throughout, or exiting, the campus.

IDENTIFYING WHO HAS BEEN AFFECTED BY THE CRISIS

Before rendering crisis intervention, support providers should identify the segment of the population that has been affected. For example, if a student in a self-contained exceptional education class is very ill, the response may be localized to that class. If a band member is battling a serious illness, the emotional impact might be limited mostly to the band members themselves. In contrast, if a very visible, popular student is critically injured, a greater portion of the school population might be affected.

Slaikeu (1990, as cited in Basham et al., 2000) constructed a tool called BASIC that assesses the level of crisis impact and determines who is in the most critical need of assistance. The acronym BASIC stands for **B**ehavioral, **A**ffective, **S**omatic, **I**nterpersonal, and **C**ognitive. For example, behavioral reactions to crisis include poor appetite, sleeplessness, and forgetfulness. Each category's symptoms are ranked on a scale of 1 through 10.

1	2	3	4	5	6	7	8	9	10
Infrequent, brief, minimal symptoms			←	→			Frequent, long-lasting, severe symptoms		

Slaikeu notes that those using the BASIC model enjoy the advantage of using the same language when indicating the impact of a crisis.

THREE CRITICAL QUESTIONS TO ADDRESS IMPACT EFFECTIVELY

After considering the aforementioned issues, crisis team leaders and administrators can more accurately answer three basic questions and make their assignments.

1. How Many Support Personnel Need to Be Mobilized?

When a call is made for a crisis intervention team to mobilize, the first question asked is, "How many members need to be activated?" Unfortunately, no formula exists regarding the precise number of interventionist necessary for specific events. Crisis team leaders and school administrators can, however, make approximate predictions regarding the number of providers necessary for a schoolwide event versus a more localized crisis affecting a smaller portion of the school population. The number of support personnel available on a campus can also affect the number of district or non-school-based interventionists mobilized. When assigning crisis intervention team members to a school, a rule of thumb is to send too many rather than too few. If too many interventionists are called to a school, the decision can always be made to dismiss personnel whose presence isn't necessary. Being understaffed could be problematic because the time necessary to mobilize additional support providers might place the school at a real disadvantage.

2. What Type of Intervention Services Will Be Necessary?

If a crisis is of a medical nature, for example, an outbreak of an airborne disease, a crisis team leader might decide to send personnel who possess a medical background, such as nurses. A principal might decide to mobilize additional school resource officers if an outbreak of violence has occurred on campus, or if a longtime, popular teacher has died, the crisis intervention team might be composed of counselors to work with grieving faculty members.

Often, crisis teams include members who specialize in specific duties. For example, a team member who is experienced with the media might be selected to conduct a television interview, or another team member might be more comfortable assisting a school administrator as an emotional announcement to their students and staff is prepared.

3. How Long Will the Crisis Team's Presence Be Necessary?

A crisis that affects the population of an entire campus might necessitate that crisis intervention personnel be available for a longer time. For non-school-based support teams, the duration of their services can be affected by the presence of existing support personnel who can continue to provide services when the crisis team exits campus.

Helpful Tips

- Identify the person(s) in charge of mobilizing the crisis response unit or team. Make sure they are aware of the importance of impact variables and the questions these variables might help answer.
- Don't commit the aforementioned impact variables to memory. Write them down!
- Invite input from other crisis team leaders or administrators before making decisions regarding impact variables. Alternative points of view can prove to be valuable when making critical decisions.

Questions for Discussion

1. Have you ever observed or been involved in a school-wide crisis (e.g., the loss of a student or faculty member, the September 11th tragedy, or Hurricane Katrina)? What was the most impressive aspect of your school's response to this situation? What could have been done differently?

2. During the most recent crisis on your campus, did you feel that the school's response was adequate? In your opinion, were there enough crisis interventionists available for the school population? Did you feel that their presence on campus was sufficient to serve the school population?

3. Does your campus or district have a school-based crisis intervention team or have access to a district crisis intervention team? Does your school have access to both types of teams? Are the aforementioned impact variables considered before these teams are mobilized?

ISSUE SIX

Non-School-Based Crisis Intervention Teams

Districts and Schools Working Together

Three days prior to the start of the winter break, three physical education classes (totaling 63 students) at Northmint Senior High School witness a small passenger airplane crash into an adjacent field. Although no students are injured, the majority of the classes hear, then watch, the aircraft plummet to the ground. School administrators quickly proceed to the field and direct the students to the auditorium. The school's five counselors and one human relations specialist also proceed to the auditorium and begin to comfort the students. News of the accident quickly spreads throughout the school's 1,950 students.

As the principal assesses the situation, he decides to contact the district's crisis intervention team. Approximately 45 minutes later, eight team members arrive at the school. The crisis team's on-site coordinator consults with the counseling department chairperson and school administrators, and asks how the school has begun to respond to what has happened and

67

the ways in which district-level interventionists can collabo-rate to extend their efforts. It is decided that a crisis team member will be paired with a school counselor for the purposes of cofacilitating each of six group-counseling sessions. Of the two remaining crisis team members, one is assigned to accom-pany and consult with the principal throughout the day. This team member subsequently engages in a variety of duties, including helping the principal write an announcement for the school population and conducting television interviews. The other crisis team member is asked to "float," or render services wherever and whenever necessary.

At the conclusion of the day, a debriefing session is con-ducted for all support providers. The principal comments on how well the district's crisis team worked with his counseling staff, and also gave him valuable personal consultation. The coun-seling and guidance department chairperson also notes that her staff was fortunate to learn new and innovative crisis inter-vention counseling techniques from the team. Two weeks later the school principal forwards a letter of appreciation to the dis-trict superintendent, citing the services of the district's crisis intervention team.

If only all intervention efforts went so well! This type of response is truly the goal for both school-based and district-level teams when they are in a position to collaborate. Unfor-tunately, many scenarios play out differently. The following vignette presents a situation in which team members do not function as smoothly.

Virgil Kenner High School, a large rural institution, enrolls 2,100 students. The principal, a former counselor, is in her second year of duty at Kenner and one of her first priorities was to establish a school-based crisis intervention team. The team is composed of the school's five counselors, a school social worker, and a school psychologist.

Early on a routine spring morning—as the principal attends an out-of-county workshop—Marilyn Smith, the assistant principal, is contacted by a local chemical processing plant located approximately one mile from the school and the site of a fatal toxic gas accident six months earlier. The plant official frantically explains that within the hour, a possible leak at the facility might threaten the school. Smith immediately initiates lockdown procedures and then contacts her area general director to inform him of the situation. Students and faculty scramble to follow procedures, but within 30 minutes the actual reason for the lockdown begins filtering down to the students and the faculty.

Forty-five minutes after his warning to the school, the plant official again contacts the administrator and informs her that the leak is contained. Numerous parents, in spite of being informed of the good news, descend on the school to retrieve their children. As a result, a chaotic situation develops in the front office and Student Affairs office. As students return to their classes, entire classrooms are identified as having emotionally traumatized students, despite being informed that no threat existed. Smith summons the district's crisis intervention team and requests additional support.

Seven members of the district's crisis intervention team arrive on the Kenner campus within an hour. Upon their arrival, the team's on-site coordinator directs his members to proceed to the media center and begin counseling students congregated at that location. The team assigns seven students to each group, then immediately initiates counseling sessions. This occurs to the dismay of the school's counseling staff, who had conducted sessions prior to the team's arrival. One crisis team member allows a student to leave campus, although no parent or guardian granted permission for her to leave the school. Another team member proceeds to the guidance suite and attempts to take charge of the students who descended on the department, to the chagrin of the guidance secretary whose preassigned role was to handle the logistical movement of students as they entered the office.

At the debriefing session at the end of day, Smith and the on-site crisis team coordinator lead a discussion of the day's proceedings. Immediately, the counseling and guidance department chairperson voices her displeasure with the district's crisis team. When asked to

(Continued)

(Continued)

elaborate, she explains that the district's team did not work in coordination with the school-based crisis team. According to the counselor, "The district team showed up, took over, and didn't consult with us on what we'd already done. We're the school's crisis team and we felt like second class citizens in our own school!" The school social worker adds, "Yes! They sure were the experts today, weren't they?"

School-based crisis intervention teams remain a very valuable tool for school districts, because they provide logistical, psychological, and ancillary crisis interventions for a multitude of turbulent events on our campuses. Ideally, every school should have an on-site crisis intervention team. In the best cases, both schools and districts have teams ready to provide multiple levels of support for students and staff during and after a crisis. But as the number of people involved in any intervention effort increases, the need for mutual understanding, respect, and collaboration increases as well.

THE MAKEUP OF DISTRICT-LEVEL TEAMS

Chapter 4 identified logical school-based crisis intervention team members based on their roles and areas of expertise in the school community. Not every school has its own counselor, social worker, *and* psychologist, so schools don't always have the full complement of mental health consultants available on site. District-level teams can fortunately offer a wider array of mental health and community professionals than many schools can provide themselves. In Volusia County, Florida, for example, the 2005/2006 district-level crisis intervention team included two team coordinators who are specialists in guidance of students with emotional disabilities. Additional team members included the district coordinator for school social work services, the district coordinator for school psychological services, two school social workers, and a school psychologist (School District of Volusia County, 2005).

Michael Pines (2001) has written an account of how the Alhambra City and High School District in California mobilized its crisis intervention team after an incident at Ramona Elementary School. Pines recounts that, during an otherwise normal school day, a severely disabled and well-loved sixth-grade student fell unconscious during class. The child received CPR and, after being taken to the hospital, was pronounced dead. Only one school psychologist—who knew the student well—had been assigned to the school. According to Pines:

> The principal knew that the psychologist alone could not help everyone so she requested additional mental health resources from the District Crisis Intervention Team. . . . The team consisted of 40 school psychologists, nurses, and counselors. In addition, help was requested from the Safe Schools Center where staff was immediately mobilized along with staff from the Los Angeles County Department of Mental Health. Also summoned were school-based mental health resources from the Almansor Center, Asian Pacific Counseling Center, and the California School of Professional Psychology that provides services to schools in the district. (p. 1)

Not all schools and districts have these resources accessible, but it's important to keep in mind that great tragedies require great help. The large numbers of district-level staff who may converge on a crisis scene underscores the need for collaborative procedures to be put in place.

ADVANTAGES AND DISADVANTAGES OF DISTRICT-LEVEL CRISIS INTERVENTION TEAMS

There are several advantages to forming district-level crisis intervention teams. First, their members generally receive specialized crisis intervention training. Their expertise can be shared with school-based support providers who may not have had the opportunity to secure this concentrated training.

District team members can also maintain a degree of objectivity, as they often have little familiarity with the victims of the crisis.

Regarding disadvantages, the nature of a crisis and availability of school-based support personnel usually dictates the duration of a district team's presence on a campus (see Chapter 7). Most teams exit a campus within one to four days. This can make assimilation into the milieu difficult. A lack of knowledge of the physical aspects of a campus and of members of the school population are also obstacles that remain especially challenging. In addition, another major obstacle for district-level teams is the lack of familiarity with school-based support personnel. This might result in problems relating to the coordination of support activities and could affect the quality of their intervention.

THREE GUIDELINES FOR NON-SCHOOL-BASED/DISTRICT CRISIS TEAMS

The vignettes at the beginning of this chapter dramatically illustrate two distinct approaches by the respective district crisis intervention teams. In the first vignette, the district's crisis team entered the campus and blended well with the existing school-based crisis intervention team. No compatibility issues were apparent and the school-based guidance staff acknowledged the team for its innovative techniques.

In contrast, the district's team in the second vignette did very little to endear itself to existing support personnel, and to say the least, the combination of the two units didn't make for a good mix. Let's examine several issues that identify the perceptions of school-based personnel and how district-level teams can put their best foot forward.

1. Avoid a Cavalry Approach

If a non-school-based crisis intervention team views itself as the school's sole source of relief and support, the team places itself at a real disadvantage. Though the unit might rightfully feel confident in its skills, chances are school-based personnel with whom they come in contact might feel otherwise. This was evident in the second vignette. Crisis teams (whether school-based or non-school-based) are not the "cavalry" and should avoid gaining this reputation at all cost. Emotionally affected students and staff are usually truly appreciative for the support they receive, but a cavalry approach works against the goal of the non-school-based crisis intervention team's successfully coordinating their efforts with existing school-based staff. Nobody wants to feel upstaged, especially by another professional who isn't a regular staff member at a school.

From the moment they form and organize their mission statement, non-school-based crisis teams would be wise to adopt the philosophy that their role is to provide additional support, not replace the existing support. Adhering to this philosophy can make the difference between successful interventions and tumultuous presences on campuses whenever these non-school-based teams are activated. Very rarely have I observed school-based support providers become disgruntled or disgusted with a non-school-based crisis team if their members gradually and nonthreateningly assimilated themselves into the school environment. On the other hand, an overbearing crisis team with members who overlook school-based personnel or ignore their expertise might cause friction between the two parties. The team's arrival will be viewed with disdain, or worse, the team may not be activated in cases where their presence might have benefited a school in distress.

Crisis team leaders or supervisors are in an ideal position to promote the image of their crisis team. These leaders have the opportunity to describe what their personnel will and will not be responsible for prior to the team's entering a campus. This can be most practically achieved by the team leader simply contacting the school's site administrator prior to their arrival on campus. Crisis team leaders can also make presentations to school boards or district administrative personnel to explain their team's roles and expectations. These presentations are also good opportunities for crisis team leaders to once again emphasize their team's philosophy, which should be to *provide support for a school, not to replace the school's existing support personnel!*

2. Seek the Assistance and Expertise of School-Based Personnel Already In Place

During crisis situations, schools often employ a variety of personnel and other support professionals who possess a wealth of skill and talent in the area of crisis intervention. Both instructional and noninstructional personnel (e.g., school resource officers, office workers, custodians) have extensive knowledge of both school operations and students. These staff members should not be overlooked when the district-level crisis intervention team is summoned to a campus. As Schonfeld and Newgass (2003) point out,

> Staff members have an ongoing relationship with and knowledge of the students, their parents, and the community. This gives school personnel valuable insight and perspective that will be helpful when they screen crisis victims and intervene on their behalf. In addition, school staff will remain in the community throughout the long recovery period that follows many crises. . . . Therefore, an effective response to a large-scale crisis when well-trained school response teams are in place should rely on experts from outside the school community to provide short-term consultation but not to assume the primary response role. (p. 2)

As stated in previous chapters, a crisis response is a schoolwide effort and a wide variety of personnel should be utilized in addition to outside support teams. Rarely, if ever, is the presence of a district crisis team alone sufficient to address all the needs of a school in crisis. When a crisis team arrives on campus, it should first assess the level of capability of the existing support staff. If the staff's level of experience is low, then the district team might assume more of a leadership role; however, if the school personnel's level of experience is significant, then the district team should be sensitive to this fact and make extra effort to work in the specific direction that the school-based personnel have requested. For example, the non-school-based crisis intervention team might be asked to provide more counseling services than consultation with the administration and teachers. As a rule of thumb, district crisis teams should assume a low profile when entering a campus unless the site-based team is nonexistent or severely under-staffed. This ensures a nonthreatening presence, and as a result, might increase school-based personnel's willingness to coordinate intervention support with the team.

3. Recognize That the District Team Is Not the Sole Provider of Services

School districts often rely solely on the services of a district-based team for crisis intervention support, especially in the area of psychological support. Ironically, this occurs despite most schools' employing personnel and additional student services personnel who have taken graduate course-work in the areas of counseling and psychology, though possibly not in the area of school crisis intervention. Such personnel can be easily called on during crisis situations in which portions of the school population seek support.

Guidance and counseling services—and additional, avail-able services from school social workers, school psychologists, and human relationships specialists—should be expected and valued, because in most cases providers of such services remain well equipped to address the emotional needs of students and faculty. Many times, their expertise in the area of crisis intervention can be equivalent or even greater than that of non-school-based intervention team members. Diversity is a real plus during crisis intervention activities (Center for Mental Health in Schools at UCLA, 2005), and the talents of existing school-based personnel should not be overlooked by district or non-school-based crisis intervention teams. According to Basham, Appleton, and Dykeman (2000), nonclassified support staff, including bus drivers, food preparation/ serving staff, and maintenance personnel, provide significant assistance during school emergencies. They remain familiar with the campus and are often acquainted with staff and students. As the crisis situation is stabilized, their involvement is essential to assisting in the normalization of the school.

The presence of non-school-based crisis intervention teams certainly benefits schools, but at no time should these teams work in opposition to existing school-based crisis interventionists. If this occurs, team leaders must immediately review and identify the circumstances that brought the teams into conflict, if progress toward addressing school needs is to occur.

Helpful Tips

- Be acquainted with the procedures for accessing your district's non-school-based crisis intervention team. Do you know the names of district contact persons and their telephone numbers? Don't wait for a crisis to occur before learning this valuable information!
- Whether the unit is school-based or non-school-based, emphasize the importance of working together and coordinating activities with other crisis intervention personnel that might be included in future support efforts.

Questions for Discussion

1. Have you ever provided crisis intervention support in conjunction with a non-school-based (district) crisis intervention team? Did this outside team blend in with the services that you and your colleagues were providing? If not, why?

2. To what degree does your district or school rely on non-school-based crisis intervention support? Do you feel that most schools in your district can adequately address the needs of traumatized faculty and staff "in house" or without the services of outside support?

3. In your opinion, what are the main advantages of having a non-school-based crisis intervention team at your school's disposal? If your district doesn't have a team, what has prevented its formation?

Teachers

The Overlooked Interventionists

On a late September school day, a tornado touches down on the physical education field at Green Forest Elementary School. Numerous students observe the tornado from their classroom windows as they hurriedly engage in emergency procedures. Most of the students in the school hear the ominous sound of the tornado as it passed close to the campus.

After the tornado dissipates, the students are allowed to return to their classrooms. Teachers in the primary grades immediately notice that students are frightened and clingy. After assessing the damage to the campus, the principal, Tom Dunstorn, requests that the school counselor and administrators visit every classroom to assess the level of emotional trauma. He also contacts the district's crisis intervention team to request their presence at the school. The principal is informed that most classrooms require some degree of crisis intervention. Unfortunately, dismissal is only 45 minutes away and frantic parents have begun to converge of the campus to remove their children from school. The crisis team has yet to arrive and the teachers are asked to stabilize their classrooms. An afterschool emergency faculty meeting is also announced.

After a delayed dismissal and chaos in the front office, Dunstorn begins the faculty meeting 45 minutes late, which is understandable considering the day's events. First, the administrator thanks the faculty for their actions during the emergency. Next, the newly arrived crisis intervention team is introduced. The principal explains that the team and support personnel will visit each class on the following school day. Dunstorn also asks that any faculty member who needs to speak to a crisis team member for debriefing or consultation purposes do so after the meeting is adjourned.

A first-grade teacher raises her hand. "With all due respect to the crisis team, wouldn't it be better if our students worked with their own teachers? After all, they are our kids and we're pretty sensitive to their emotions." The teacher continues, "I do, of course, realize that special preparation is necessary to do this type of work, but if we were trained. . . ." Dunstorn steps in, "That's a great question, but I think you hit the nail on the head. It might just actually be a training issue." The principal then indicates that this topic will be placed on the agenda of the next steering committee meeting.

That teacher really brings up an interesting point. Why aren't teachers encouraged to become more involved in school crisis intervention efforts? In fact, for decades teachers have interacted with students who reeled from traumatic events. Classroom-based educators have long taken opportunities to stop classes to discuss emotionally laden events such as President Kennedy's assassination, the Challenger disaster, the Columbine school shootings, and more recently, the events of September 11th and Hurricane Katrina. These situations certainly warranted discussion for students old enough to be aware of what had transpired. What hasn't been established, however, is the role of the classroom teacher as a provider of psychological support. Chapter 1 discussed reasons why school personnel sometimes refuse or hesitate to become involved in crisis intervention efforts, including a lack of training, liability issues, or the task of crisis intervention not being contained in a job description. However, for the purposes of this chapter, let's assume that teachers, like the one at Green Forest Elementary, have a desire to become involved in crisis intervention efforts. What stops them? Historically, why haven't classroom instructors been more prominent with regard to the provision of psychological support within their own classrooms?

WHAT PREVENTS TEACHER INVOLVEMENT IN CRISIS INTERVENTION?

Expectations of Roles

Ask most educators to identify the first option for school crisis intervention and in all likelihood their answer would be "our school counselor(s)." Many staff members assume important roles during a crisis, but few staff members have as large a responsibility as those providing support services, such as counselors, social workers, nurses, and often school psychologists. Few, if any, staff members are more prepared to meet the needs of emotionally stricken students and staff. We have come to rely on these personnel to address the psychological difficulties that stem from crises, and fortunately, on most occasions and in most schools, they do a great job.

There has also been an increased reliance on crisis intervention teams in recent years, which might unintentionally work against the inclusion of teachers in the crisis support process. As crises occur, these specialized teams (either school-based or district-level) are often sent to campuses with the intention of psychologically stabilizing the schools. Similar to student support personnel, however, the presence of crisis intervention teams might inadvertently preclude teachers from providing crisis intervention assistance themselves. Unfortunately, as crisis team members interact with students, classroom instructors can be cast into the role of observer rather than an active support provider. Teachers can join other crisis interventionists, however, in helping students deal with their reactions via different class activities. Teachers should never be "on the outside looking in" regarding crisis intervention because they remain much too valuable an asset during these difficult times.

Although school administrators and support personnel often overlook teachers as frontline crisis intervention providers, teachers frequently contribute to this situation as well. Often, teachers adopt the attitude, "I get paid to teach, not counsel" and thus crisis intervention is considered a duty better left to other school personnel. Though this view is understandable, many teachers also desire to participate in the crisis intervention process, but for several reasons don't.

One major factor related to the inclusion of teachers in crisis support efforts is the prevailing attitude of the administration at the school. For instance, if a principal maintains that crisis support within the school will be delivered by traditional interventionists (i.e., nurses, counselors, school social workers, and school psychologists), then, in fact, the teacher may have little to say about the issue because, in all likelihood, the necessary crisis response training will not be provided for the teacher. However, an administrator who is amenable to the possibility of teachers becoming actively involved will take the necessary steps to ensure that adequate crisis intervention training is secured for them. A first step to ensure that teachers are invited to become involved with in-class crisis intervention efforts is for these instructors to inform their administrators that they welcome the opportunity to provide this important service.

A Teacher Checklist

Teachers who chose to become involved in school crisis intervention should do the following:

- Possess a genuine willingness to become involved in the provision of school crisis intervention services, and feel that they can offer a valuable service to their students
- Be aware of the obstacles that might prevent the provision of classroom crisis intervention (e.g., an administration that refuses to permit teacher intervention) and have a desire to overcome these obstacles

- Be willing to receive crisis intervention training
- Notify their administrators if adequate crisis intervention training opportunities are not available in their school or district
- Be amenable to a team approach to school crisis intervention and remain cognizant that these interventions can involve both school-based and non-school-based personnel

THE PROVISION OF IN-CLASS CRISIS INTERVENTION

I addressed the issue of teachers and in-class crisis response in a research study that examined the extent to which teachers viewed the provision of crisis intervention as part of their role in the classroom setting (Jaksec, Dedrick, & Weinberg, 2000). A survey was sent to 45 schools in a West Central Florida school district enrolling 39,483 students, and 926 ($n = 926$) teachers responded.

Though previous studies examined teachers' acceptability as it related to behavioral classroom interventions, little research had been conducted that specifically addressed elementary, middle, and secondary teachers' attitudes regarding the provision of in-class crisis intervention.

Regarding their experiences with crisis-related situations, 47% of the teachers reported that they'd had contact with students who endured crisis situations on two or more occasions during the past year. Examples of crises included:

- Homicide of a classmate
- Suicide of a classmate
- Accidental death or injury of a classmate
- News of a tragedy
- Indirect/direct threat from the community (e.g., gang-related activity)

In addition, 77% of the teachers reported that they were aware of students within their classroom who had reacted to news of a tragedy on one or more occasions. It was apparent that these teachers were indeed exposed to students who may have felt the repercussions of emotionally traumatic events, so I then explored their levels of actual crisis intervention activity with these students. I found that 60% of the teachers had provided two or more crisis intervention services within their classrooms in the past year. Those interventions included class discussions, writing exercises, consultation, and group or individual counseling. Class discussions were implemented by 75% of the teachers on at least one occasion, and 31% of the teachers used writing exercises on at least one occasion. While 32% of the teachers on at least one occasion consulted with other professionals, such as school counselors, regarding student reactions to trauma, 34% of the teachers conducted at least one group counseling session on at least one occasion, and 63% engaged in individual counseling with students.

It was clear that teachers had intervened with their students who had experienced a crisis. I further learned that 41% of the teachers attended at least one crisis intervention workshop, but only 16% attended two or more workshops. Only 17% of the teachers attended a crisis intervention workshop within the past year and 13% in the past two years. Unfortunately, 59% of the teachers had never attended a crisis intervention workshop. Though teacher involvement was clearly apparent, their necessary training was not!

The results of this study indicated that teachers actually displayed a high level of acceptance regarding the provision of in-class crisis intervention services. With this in mind, school districts might be well advised to provide thorough crisis intervention training for their teachers. It would serve to benefit both the teachers and their students.

THE CASE FOR TEACHERS AS CRISIS INTERVENTIONISTS

We've looked at several reasons why many teachers aren't involved in in-class crisis intervention services and have learned that many teachers do want to become involved in intervention efforts. We've also noted that teacher training in crisis intervention for the most part was insufficient. But why broach this topic and why should teachers even be bothered with dealing with traumatized students? There are several reasons.

Familiarity Versus the "Stranger" Complex

When children are injured while playing, their first reaction is usually to seek their parents for help. Why? Because their parents are a very familiar and natural source of comfort and assistance.

Elementary school teachers have contact with their students for six hours or more per day. At the middle and secondary school level, teachers usually see their students daily. As a result of this familiarity, teachers eventually become well aware of their student's behaviors and overall emotional makeup. Most teachers are also cognizant of their students' moods, and as a result remain in a great position to observe their reactions as they respond to a crisis. Therefore, it makes sense for teachers to be one of the main sources of psychological support (not therapy) for their students.

This is not to say that support personnel unfamiliar with students cannot effectively deliver help to them when they are traumatized. Knowledgeable and sensitive interventionists probably will encounter few problems establishing the rapport necessary to provide effective crisis intervention. Situations do arise, however, when students feel uncomfortable with a stranger, and no matter how adept the interventionist, the provision of services can be hindered. This problem is alleviated when the teacher is in a position to provide crisis intervention or other classroom activities. Other than their parents, who knows the students better?

The Issue of Manpower

In some school districts, the absence of crisis support personnel can become a genuine issue for schools in distress. The addition of teachers as crisis interventionists lessens the burden on undermanned schools and their districts. Though small-scale crises are usually handled easily by existing crisis personnel, large-scale events, as experienced by the students of Green Forest Elementary School, might fittingly lend themselves to the involvement of teachers.

Even in the temporary absence of regular crisis intervention personnel, a teacher who has the opportunity to receive crisis intervention training can at least temporarily address the needs of the class until regular support personnel are available.

Bonding and Trust

We've often heard that individuals who see each other through particularly difficult times tend to bond emotionally. These individuals also establish significant levels of trust with one another: "We got through it together!" This is one of the few positives to emerge from traumatic situations.

Teachers always seek ways in which to connect with their students and establish rapport and trust. A crisis is an opportune time for this to occur, as the teacher provides necessary support and "is there" for the students. As the crisis passes, the trust established during the difficult time often remains, and the nature of the student-teacher relationship may continue to strengthen. Students might also come to view their teachers in a more favorable light, as postcrisis they are seen as empathetic care providers.

Tracking and Follow Up

A very important part of any crisis response is the period that follows the initial intervention(s). Days, weeks, or months after an emotionally charged event, students might still exhibit maladaptive behaviors due to their inability to deal with the crisis. Unfortunately, non-school-based crisis intervention teams usually aren't available for extended periods postcrisis. Therefore, school personnel assume the responsibility of addressing persisting concerns.

Teachers are in an advantageous position to observe students after a crisis, but the teacher often isn't present during the initial crisis and support period. So, it remains difficult for them to monitor or assess the progress or deterioration of the student's behavior. Conversely, a teacher who is in a position to render crisis intervention support from the onset of the event, and eventually observes the student experiencing post-crisis difficulties, can then refer the student for additional support from other personnel, such as the school counselor, school social worker, nurse, or school psychologist. Involvement from the inception of the crisis allows teachers to more easily monitor the progress or deterioration of their students.

ADMINISTRATIVE STEPS FOR TEACHER INCLUSION IN CRISIS INTERVENTION ACTIVITIES

1. To gauge the level of teacher interest in crisis intervention, the principal or site administrator could broach the topic at a faculty meeting. The meeting should preferably be held during the preplanning period at the beginning of the school year.

2. If possible, arrange teacher inservice training sessions early in the school year. These sessions can be conducted by experienced school or district-level personnel. In addition, community-based or university-based personnel could be considered for teacher trainings.

3. Teachers who choose to become involved in school crisis intervention response should have an opportunity to be observed by experienced crisis interventionists and/or cofacilitate activities with these interventionists. This provides guidance and increases the teacher's knowledge of crisis intervention.

4. If teachers choose to provide crisis intervention activities within their classrooms, they also should have the opportunity to debrief or discuss their interventions after they are provided.

Helpful Tips

- Practical lessons and class discussions are realistic options for teachers as crisis situations affect their classrooms. At the elementary level, play, reenactment, puppets, art, and discussion group reading and writing are viable crisis intervention activities. At the junior high school and high school levels, teachers could consider homeroom class discussions, creative writing, literature, and peer listening activities (Center for Mental Health in Schools at UCLA, 2005).
- Schools should offer consultation and solicit feedback from teachers after they have engaged in classroom crisis intervention in an effort to build on their experiences.
- Teachers should be aware of all resources and additional support personnel available for their students if they require additional support as the result of a crisis.

Questions for Discussion

1. Should teachers have the opportunity to provide crisis intervention services? Explain your answer.

2. Are you familiar with teachers who have provided crisis intervention in their classrooms? Where did they receive their training?

3. In which ways are teachers particularly well suited to provide in-class crisis intervention? Explain your answer.

Did We Forget Anyone?

Addressing the Needs of Every Staff Member

Joe Mendez has been employed as a janitor at Sunnydale Elementary School for approximately 24 years. A slightly built man in his late 60s, Mendez has made a habit of adopting several underprivileged families and providing for them during the Christmas holidays. It is one of the many charitable acts Mendez performs during every school year. As is his style, he shies away from any type of special recognition for his efforts and goes about his charity work with little fanfare or publicity. Throughout his years at Sunnydale, parents, staff, and students, have come to know Mendez as somewhat of an institution at the school, so much so that many former students who progressed through Sunnydale Elementary have made a habit of returning for a brief visit with "Joe the Janitor."

Early in the school year, Mendez "adopted" yet another family who had been forced from their residence in another state due to a natural disaster. He grew especially fond of this particular family, who were always very thankful for his benevolence. Several times during the school week, the family's youngest son, a personable fourth grader, would make a habit of peeking around the corner of his classroom toward the jani- tor's office and offer a friendly wave to Mendez.

Early one morning, Mendez hears the tragic news that this family has been involved in a serious car accident. The fourth- grade boy is in critical condition with paralysis of his legs. Three members of the district's crisis intervention team join the school's guidance counselor in an effort to provide support for the child's classmates and teacher. Although, in all likelihood, Mendez would have politely declined the offer to talk to a stranger about the situation, he is especially upset with this news. He had experienced several tragedies during his long tenure at the school, but on this occasion he tells a fellow main- tenance worker that he might have welcomed the opportunity to at least talk about the boy and his family.

Toward the end of the school day, the principal calls a brief emergency meeting to discuss the situation with her faculty. After the meeting, the principal makes her way to her car. As she exits the parking lot, she spots Joe Mendez in her rearview mirror emptying trash into a dumpster. She immediately realizes that she neglected to invite Mendez and the school's noninstructional staff to the faculty meeting and feels an over- whelming sense of remorse. On the drive home, the principal keeps asking herself, "How could I have forgotten Joe?"

On the majority of occasions, the focus of school crisis intervention efforts is directed toward the student population. One the other hand, there is also a real concern for certain pro- fessionals who function on the periphery or even in the mid- dle of a crisis. Unfortunately (and unintentionally), these staff members are sometimes overlooked during the provision of crisis intervention support efforts. Of course, many of these faculty members choose not to receive support, and that remains their option. However, some staff members, like Joe Mendez, are affected to the degree that they welcome support that is, unfortunately, not forthcoming. Members of the nonstudent population who might require crisis intervention support include teachers and administrators, as well as non-instructional staff, including paraprofessionals and the crisis interventionists themselves.

Why Faculty Members Don't Always Receive Support

Throughout my experiences as a school crisis intervention team member, I've had many opportunities to observe staff members as they attempted to comprehend and emotionally recover from the news of a tragedy or an incident that involved a student or colleague. Many of these individuals shared significant relationships with the victim. I noticed early in my career that teachers and administrators were sometimes overlooked during the provision of support. At times, however, these staff members also refused or hesitated to receive crisis intervention services for several interesting reasons, which are discussed below.

Reason One: You Can't Help What You Don't "See"

During a crisis response, especially one involving a large portion of the school population, interventionists often find themselves scrambling in an effort to provide services to large portions of the student population. Time limits—that is, the confines of regular school hours—and the sheer number of students and/or staff requesting services often interfere with the identification of faculty members who are in need of support. Compounding this problem is the fact that these individuals often function away from the student population who receive the majority of attention. Cafeteria workers, janitors, and teachers, particularly, perform their duties outside the "line of sight" of crisis interventionists and are occasionally overlooked in regard to crisis support.

Overlooking support to a member(s) of the nonstudent population is rarely intentional. One can hope, however, this oversight occurs only once, and when subsequent crises occur, every member of the school population will have an opportunity to receive support if it's requested or required. Of course, the responsibility for inviting *all* staff members (both school-based and non-school-based) to receive support ultimately rests on school administrators or team leaders who oversee crisis intervention efforts.

Crisis interventionists and their team leaders should gauge the emotional well-being of every faculty and staff member during the school day. This serves to ensure that no individual falls through the cracks and has to emotionally endure the situation without support that ironically is readily available on the school site! Crisis team leaders and school administrators might take the opportunity to discuss this important issue during preplanning meetings that are usually held prior to the provision of crisis intervention services.

Recommendation: Prior to the provision of services, staff members should be assured that they can receive crisis intervention support if they choose. This can be communicated to the faculty via e-mail, note, or announcement (written or verbal). Crisis support personnel can also ensure that all faculty members are at least considered for support by quickly reviewing a list of personnel that can be provided by the school administration.

Reason Two: Old-Fashioned Stubbornness

On occasion, crisis interventionists will approach school personnel with the offer of support, only to hear, "No thanks, we've managed to survive to this point and we'll sure survive this!" or "Since I started teaching 29 years ago I never had anyone counsel me and I made it just fine!" However seemingly archaic some staff members' attitudes may be toward assistance, it remains those staff members' prerogative to decline support. It is conceivable that the faculty member might perceive support as a sign of weakness or vulnerability. Though the crisis interventionist's offer of support is genuine, it's also important for these personnel to remain sensitive to the fact that their colleagues may be nonreceptive to crisis support for a variety of reasons. Nevertheless, it can be frustrating for the interventionist because his or her colleagues could benefit from valuable support during these difficult situations.

Recommendation: Don't coerce the reluctant staff member into accepting support. Rather, offer support and inform the individual of your possible whereabouts during the day and your willingness to assist if and when he or she agrees to it.

Reason Three: "I've Got to Be There for My Kids"

At the elementary school level, teachers are in contact with all of their students for most of the school day. At the middle and secondary school level, teachers see their students daily, and some teachers have contact with the same students on numerous occasions during the school day. During the school year, student-teacher relationships are eventually formed as the teacher gains familiarity with the student. Likewise, administrators form relationships with colleagues and students. They too gain a familiarity with individuals who unfortunately might be the eventual victims of a tragedy.

Teachers and administrators can be affected greatly by a tragedy or unfortunate event, but they may choose to remain on duty while they struggle to sort out their feelings regarding the situation. It's admirable for teachers or administrators to willingly remain with their classes or remain on duty in lieu of receiving support. Often, the same reasoning is heard: "I just wanted to be there with my staff."

Though the value of support is undeniable, a teacher can't be forced to leave his or her classroom to receive support, and an administrator can't be ordered to talk to someone. Their desire to remain with their students or colleagues is genuine, and their intentions should be respected regardless of their reasoning. Crisis interventionists should, however, make a note that though teachers or administrators may not initially opt for support, they might decide that support is a good idea later in the day or week. It's imperative that staff members never be forgotten once their original intentions are voiced. Interventionists can reconnect with school staff later in the day—possibly during their off-duty or lunch breaks—after their desire to be with their students has been met. This ensures that the interventionist is there for these individuals if they finally decide to request support.

Recommendation: Don't argue with teachers regarding their desire to remain with the classroom. Do, however, make sure you reconnect with them later in the day as the teacher's schedule might then allow him or her to be more agreeable to support.

Reason Four: Being Emotionally Exposed

Maybe the biggest reason for teachers or administrators to refuse to accept support is that they feel they will have a difficult time "recovering" from the emotions expressed during the contact with the crisis interventionist, particularly after a counseling session. This perceived vulnerability and threat of exposing their emotions might cause trepidation when these staff members are faced with the task of returning to their classrooms or administrative duties. In other words, staff members feel that it's better not to "let the emotional dam break." On one hand, this is a legitimate concern for teachers and administrators on strict schedules that necessitate they remain at the forefront of activities during the school day. On the other hand, those same faculty members might suffer the consequences of not having an opportunity to discuss the situation if they refuse support. Even if faculty members guard their own emotions in an effort to continue their responsibilities, crisis interventionists have several options to ensure that support is eventually provided.

Recommendation One: Wait for the staff member to have a break or off-duty period during the day. Caution should be exercised, however, because the teacher might feel that he or she is on a restricted time schedule and still hesitate to accept the invitation for support. In this instance, it might be preferable for the interventionist to invite the staff member to meet after school, after daily responsibilities are met and the fear of having emotions exposed have decreased. As mentioned earlier, interventionists should remain cognizant of each of their invitations for support and never fail to recontact the faculty member at the conclusion of the school day, if they have committed to do so.

Recommendation Two: Invite the faculty member to join in the intervention that is being conducted with another portion of the school population. For example, a teacher who is hesitant to let his or her guard down in an individual counseling session might be more receptive if he or she were included in a classroom activity. Similarly, a school administrator could be invited to attend a small-group assembly of students or other faculty members. In these settings, hesitant school personnel have the option of participating or just observing the intervention.

Reason Five: "We Aren't Really Faculty Members"

It's conceivable that noninstructional personnel, such as custodial staff, paraprofessionals, bus drivers, office personnel, and cafeteria workers, might hesitate to seek crisis intervention support because they feel that they are not a part of the regular school faculty. Like our friend Joe Mendez, noninstructional personnel certainly do share relationships with their colleagues and students, thus every effort to dispel the misperception that they're not included in crisis support efforts should be made from the highest levels of the school administration. When this misconception is corrected, then *every* faculty member will have the opportunity to receive support if necessary.

Recommendation: School administrators, specifically, should ensure that every member of their staff realizes that he or she is a valuable member of the faculty and, as such, has the opportunity to receive support when necessary. Staff members should be informed of this option before a crisis occurs, optimally at meetings dedicated to crisis intervention planning.

Reason Six: "I Was Too Busy Helping People"

The provision of crisis intervention can be fatiguing and performed under the most chaotic of circumstances. On occasion, support providers are preoccupied with their duties to the extent that they forget to receive support for themselves during the day or at the conclusion of the school day. This is unfortunate because the debriefing process is a critical component for the crisis interventionist. Crisis interventionists should not be responsible for conducting their debriefing sessions; rather, this task should be the direct responsibility of the crisis team leader or school administrator.

Recommendations: Crisis team administrators should regularly observe team members during the crisis and temporarily relieve these individuals of their duties if the situation necessitates. This ensures that the interventionist has the opportunity to debrief due to any number of circumstances, including physical or emotional fatigue.

Helpful Tips

- Discussing the availability of support for all staff members prior to a crisis makes accepting support at the time of crisis much easier. Faculty meetings dedicated to crisis planning are a great time to discuss this important staff option.
- Remember that school personnel often refuse crisis intervention support for myriad reasons. Though their rationale for not receiving support might be confounding to the interventionist, these reasons are valid to those faculty members and should be respected as such. Through patience and preplanning on behalf of

the interventionist, these faculty members can eventually receive the support that they require.

- On occasion, it might be advisable for an instructor to be removed from a classroom due to their emotionality related to the situation. If, however, a teacher indicates that he or she intends to remain in the classroom, school administrative personnel might assure the instructor that classroom coverage can be provided if necessary. The administrator—along with the interventionist—can assure the instructor that the obligation to return to the classroom is contingent on the staff member's capability of resuming his or her duties. This ensures that the faculty member doesn't feel rushed back to the classroom, and as a result, the staff member feels more comfortable.

Questions for Discussion

1. Have you ever been involved in the provision of crisis intervention services when the needs of noninstructional support personnel were overlooked? If so, was the oversight intentional or unintentional? Was this oversight addressed?

2. In your opinion, what is the most effective way to address the emotional needs of a staff member? Leave the staff member alone and return later during the day? Invite the staff member to join in crisis intervention activities (e.g., the teacher remains in the classroom with students)? Or suggest that the staff member leave the venue to receive support?

3. After the provision of crisis intervention, do you usually have the opportunity to debrief? What importance do you place on a crisis interventionist's opportunity to debrief?

Primary Prevention

Preparing for Crises Before They Happen

Secondary school guidance counselor Jerome Dawson gained a reputation as a staff member who gladly accepted the opportunity to engage in crisis intervention when necessary. During his career, Dawson had become quite adept at progressive crisis intervention techniques and his talent was often necessary since Larson Senior High School had endured the deaths of five students and two faculty members during a recent two-year period. As the school reacted to these situations, both staff and students often sought Dawson's support and guidance.

During the fall semester crisis intervention team meeting, which is attended by three administrators, guidance-counseling staff, the school psychologist, and the school social worker, Dawson voices his opinion about the necessity of providing crisis intervention focused on prevention rather than reaction. He asks his colleagues if, during the past two years, the school's population, in light of its staggering string of misfortune, might have been better served if students and staff had the opportunity to discuss grief issues prior to these losses actually occurring. After a long pause, a fellow school counselor agrees that a preventive approach would benefit many individuals. Another member of the crisis team also agrees with Dawson.

The school social worker says that though she is embarrassed to admit it, preventive crisis intervention is foreign to her. She notes that most school interventionists seem to be prepared to provide support, but usually following a tragedy. She then asks, "Why would we want to teach students to attempt to deal with crises before they happen? Why fill their heads with worries about something that may never come to pass? This just doesn't make sense to me!" Another school counselor then questions the team's level of comfort should they try to engage the school population with issues or misfortunes that had yet to occur. Others on the team aren't sure how to proceed. To Dawson's frustration, the meeting concludes with no resolution or plan of action developed for initiating a primary prevention program within the school.

Despite many good and welcome innovations regarding how schools approach crisis intervention, we still tend to be reactive rather than proactive in our attempts to deal with crises. Compared to the numerous reactive crisis intervention approaches, few proactive approaches currently exist. More now than ever before, a proactive approach to school crisis intervention is necessary.

After the events of September 11, 2001, I contacted Ofra Ayalon, a renowned school crisis interventionist in Israel, to discuss the tragedy and its possible effects on our nation's students and educators. One of her first comments was, "Are you ready to listen now?" referring to our previous conversations in which she'd urged educators in the United States (and other countries) to consider a preventive approach to crisis intervention. This approach would address mounting concerns, such as terrorism, along with crises that have always affected our schools, from large-scale natural disasters that affect many people to more individual events such as bullying or a parent's death. Recognizing the necessity for crisis intervention efforts, Ayalon also emphasized that our turbulent times—as now so grossly evident—would eventually necessitate additional approaches to assisting school populations.

THE FIRST LEVEL OF
INTERVENTION IS PREVENTION

According to Gerald Caplan's (1964) model, crisis intervention occurs at three levels: primary, secondary, and tertiary. I can best give an example of the three types of intervention by simply describing the actions of a mother whose child wants to go skateboarding. The mother is in a *primary*, or *preventative*, mode when she warns her son not to skateboard without his kneepads. Her little skateboarder, though probably reluctant, may avoid a scraped knee because his mother has intervened prior to his leaving the house. If the mother has not warned her son to wear kneepads and is subsequently called outside to assist to her injured son with his scraped knee, she has reacted to his injury and is in a *secondary*, or *reactive*, mode of response. If, several days later, the boy's scraped knee continues to cause pain because it has become severely infected, the mother will seek further medical assistance for her son. She is now in the *tertiary* mode of response because additional assistance was necessary after the accident occurred.

All three levels of crisis intervention are implemented in our nation's schools, but the most common mode of intervention remains at the secondary level: When emotionally traumatized students and staff require assistance, it is rendered. Our country has likewise traditionally reacted to crises at the secondary level. For instance, when the United States was attacked on September 11, 2001, the nation responded by initiating what's commonly known as the "war on terror." But in addition to the war effort, the U.S. government began to take a more primary approach toward the protection of its citizens. Airport and waterway security was exponentially increased, and no longer did Americans take safety for granted. Schools are not, however, without prevention models, as evidenced by a number of growing programs offered in schools (e.g., Second

Step: A Violence Prevention Curriculum and Screening for Mental Health's Signs of Suicide® Program).

WHY DON'T SCHOOLS USUALLY ENGAGE IN PRIMARY PREVENTION?

Primary crisis intervention seems to make sense, yet most schools continue to operate with the reactive mind-set to crisis: "We're ready to provide assistance once a tragedy occurs." Though this approach works effectively for many school districts, how do we know that primary intervention wouldn't benefit the school's population to an even greater degree? There are reasons for this hesitation (or refusal) to provide preventative crisis intervention.

According to Ayalon (1993, 2005), trauma, disasters, and loss are seldom considered appropriate topics for processing with school children. The tendency to carry on exists after disaster, even at the expense of ensuing repression, distortion of memories, depression, and increased aggression among the children who have been affected. Like the attitudes of adults in the general population, school personnel reflect social taboos, magical thinking, denial of anxiety, and keeping a stiff upper lip. Once reawakened, memories of loss, fear, and confusion can threaten one's self-image and sense of security.

Ayalon (1979) identified a research study that sought to explore school personnel's consent to conduct primary prevention after a severe terrorist attack in Israel. The study indicated that 63% of the personnel were against the use of primary prevention. Reasons given for the refusal included:

- Do not upset the children (children must not think about death).
- Do not disrupt the existing curriculum.
- Children should forget the bad times.
- Let sleeping dogs lie (what is over is over).
- Don't invite the devil (talking about troubles will bring them back again).

- As a child, I never had psychological intervention—and never missed it.

The study also found that 32% of school personnel were in favor of primary intervention, and provided the following reasons for their consent:

- Because children's behavior is getting out of hand (some are too depressed, some too aggressive)
- To provide   answers to children's difficult questions (about death, life after death, questioning divine justice)

THE BENEFITS OF PRIMARY PREVENTION

Ayalon (1979) notes that various researchers have identified the potential for stressful situations to function as catalysts and produce change, open barriers in rigid systems, and open channels of communication that prior to the crisis were unknown. Therefore, during early planning and assistance during a crisis, one must not only consider the fears, confusion, and helplessness that exist because of the traumatic event, but also the ability of the intervener "to use these characteristics for the intent of redirecting the elements of the system to more efficient functioning" (pp. 2, 20, 25).

In addition, Ayalon (2005) has explained that a mutual relationship exists between the entire community and a school system. A community's spirit and hardships are reflected by its schools as students and school personnel bring to the campus a full range of values, feelings, anxieties, and joys of their families on regular days and in times of stress. Students often spend more time at school than in their households, and the breakdown of the traditional family, coupled with the inability of parents to provide for their children's psychological needs, places an even greater responsibility on school personnel to tend to the needs of students. This responsibility increases after a crisis, and schools must be prepared in advance so that the structure (both organizational and educational) will not break down in an emergency. Ironically, a paradox of sorts is identified by Ayalon (1979):

> This sort of anticipatory intervention highly depends on the readiness of the system to deal with disasters during peaceful times, and to relate to past traumatic experiences and possible future threats, despite the burden that such activities may place on the system's daily functioning, and against the natural human tendency to forget past distressful events and carry on unperturbed. This paradox often impedes the intentions to implement primary prevention programs in schools and in communities despite its proven gains. (p. 3)

When it is conducted, primary crisis intervention is addressed on two levels: the organizational and the psychological (Ayalon, 1979).

Organizational Level

The organizational level prepares the school for alternative functioning in a crisis. A traumatic event may produce changes in routine or the overall balance of the school. Changes must be taken into account and alternatives must be formulated to answer questions that arise. For instance, how will the school operate with a partial staff? Or how will studies be affected if students from other classes are grouped together during a crisis? Prior to a crisis, the goals of the intervention must be identified, assignment of roles completed, and at-risk or vulnerable students identified.

Psychological Level

Teachers should be trained in simulated crisis situations and provided teaching tools that are intended for "emergency education" for use in individual and group activities for enhancement of coping activities. Ayalon (1979) emphasizes that the main goal of primary prevention is the encouragement of active coping, which is defined as "drawing on both external and internal resources to confront the external hazardous situation and deal with internal stresses triggered by it" (p. 3). She notes that the best way to improve coping activity is to achieve a balance between physical action, expressive behavior, cognitive problem solving, and stress inoculation. By combining these efforts, an effective model of coping mechanisms is represented that serves to confront both the waiting period and crisis situation itself.

MISCONCEPTIONS ABOUT A PREVENTIVE APPROACH

Few educators remain unaware of the turbulent state of global affairs. Increases in terrorist attacks and natural disasters continue to test the resolve and threaten to affect the mental makeup of the citizens of every country, including the United States. At the center of every one of these countries is its youth, most of whom receive some type of formal education. It's logical to assume that the anxieties and negative emotionality triggered by these events have trickled down to classrooms—and will continue to do so. Preventive crisis intervention is tailor-made for this situation because these threats no doubt will continue to confront our communities.

During the past several years, I've had the opportunity to speak around the country on the topic of preventive crisis intervention. Interestingly, it continues to be considered a somewhat novel idea. Many educators remain unaware that this type of intervention is not new, but simply underused. Though preventive efforts relating to suicide and drug abuse have taken on greater significance in recent years, primary prevention efforts relating to crises have gone for the most part unused. I've noticed misconceptions that support the hesitation in accepting a more preventive approach to crisis intervention in light of recent terrorist activities. Several of these include the following.

"It Can Only Happen Once"

The September 11, 2001, nightmare is a part of history that we all would like to forget, but the magnitude of the event won't let that happen soon. Unfortunately, some individuals believe that an attack of that magnitude will probably never be repeated. "We've weathered the worst imaginable," they might say, and the urgency to readjust our approaches with children—who emotionally seemed to quickly heal after 9-11—has waned. Of course, there is no way to know if terror attacks will continue, but as recent bombings in London, Madrid, and Egypt make evident, terrorism, as well as other types of traumas such as 2005's Hurricane Katrina, makes preparation for these events all the more imperative. School personnel might be well served to take this opportunity to begin this preparation.

"It Only Happens Somewhere Else"

Prior to the appalling events of 9-11 and the devastation of Hurricane Katrina, there prevailed an attitude in the United States that terrorism and catastrophic natural disasters occurred only in foreign countries. But the United States, so often spared these types of tragedies, has in recent years experienced enormous suffering on its own soil.

For decades, the Israelis have refused to wait for the inevitable and have engaged in the art of preparing students for terrorism directed against their schools. This is especially evident in northern Israel, where attacks have exacted a terrible toll on their schools. In the early to mid 1990s, as I communicated with Israeli crisis interventionists, I too was guilty of the "it only happens over there" mind-set. I agreed that the Israeli preventive model was indeed effective and necessary, but the reality at the time was that the United States shared no borders with hostile countries. Naïve as it sounds now, we surely had no concerns about incoming mortar attacks, or terrorist activities on "our turf." How things changed in a very short time! The use of the Israeli prevention model, which until recently was rarely adapted for use in our country, is now easily conceivable.

I echo Ayalon's words: "Are we ready to listen yet?"

"Schools Are Off Limits!"

It has always been unthinkable that anyone—even terrorists—would dare to intentionally harm schoolchildren. Certainly, we thought, school campuses have been—and will always be—off limits to intentional acts of destruction, but for decades Israel has suffered through events that have demonstrated that this isn't necessarily true. Many of us also clearly remember, with horror, the Beslan school hostage crisis of September 2004, when Chechen terrorists overtook School Number One in Beslan, Russia. According to a BBC news article ("Putin Meets Angry Beslan Mothers," 2005), 186 children died during the three-day occupation. Terrorism knows no boundaries regarding age, sex, or venue. As ominous as this fact remains, it also serves as a wake-up call for educators to better prepare for something that we shudder to think ever possible: the targeting of our schools.

LOOKING FORWARD

Preparing for a crisis during peaceful times is something that remains foreign to personnel in the majority of our nation's schools. The implementation of a different crisis intervention approach will require the altering of existing mind-sets. The inclusion of primary prevention can only serve to profit students who will have to endure the psychological ramifications of crises that will inevitably occur in an increasingly volatile world. Ultimately, school administrators will have to take the lead in the efforts to shift toward a preventative approach to crisis intervention. At first, this choice may not be popular, and it will be considered unorthodox. Patience and the ability to be receptive to new intervention techniques will also be required, because it's often difficult to attempt interventions that go against what is both comfortable and familiar. Maintaining a reactive approach regarding the provision of crisis intervention services will serve only to prevent students from acquiring a learned resourcefulness that might enable them to deal with impending dangers more effectively.

Helpful Tips

- Become acquainted with the three levels of crisis intervention. An excellent resource is Gerald Caplan's book, *Principle's of Preventative Psychiatry* (1964).
- Discuss with your colleagues the possibility of engaging in preventative-level crisis intervention. Include in your discussion the pros and cons of a proactive approach.

Questions for Discussion

1. Is preventative crisis intervention implemented in your school district? If not, do you feel that your district would be amenable to this approach?

2. In your opinion, what are some of the obstacles regarding the implementation of primary prevention?

3. Considering the volatility of global affairs, do you feel that primary prevention should become more prevalent in our nation's schools?

Conclusion

As evidenced by the tragedies that took place in late 2006 in Nickel Mines, Pennsylvania, and Bailey, Colorado, and the numerous other events that affect the normal functioning of our nation's schools on a daily basis, it's easy to see that crisis intervention remains an important tool for school personnel.

Though any number of topics could have been considered for inclusion in *Toward Successful School Crisis Intervention*, the specific issues in this book were selected because they consistently manifest themselves as significant factors that can determine the success or failure of school crisis intervention. These issues were also selected based on my—and other school personnel's—actual experiences during crisis-related situations, as well as having the opportunity to observe how these issues affect school crisis intervention attempts.

By allowing the reader to recognize and address the topics contained in *Toward Successful School Crisis Intervention*, I hope the amount of unnecessary effort expended during an already challenging task will decrease and the overall quality of the school crisis intervention will increase.

School crisis intervention can be a very rewarding job, if certain pitfalls are avoided and interventionists do not proceed headlong into the task unprepared. Having the opportunity to participate in preplanning and training is crucial. In addition, being cognizant of certain (though somewhat less obvious) issues related to the field is also imperative and cannot help but increase the effectiveness of these crisis interventionists.

This book should assist you and your colleagues as you prepare for tragedies of varying scale and the recovery efforts that will have such a lasting impact on students, schools, and communities.

Common Questions and Helpful Answers About Group Counseling Sessions

The following questions are often asked by professionals who have been frustrated when engaged in crisis counseling interventions.

Question: "How could I have stopped some group members from talking during my counseling session? Some of the kids were so quiet, but a few just wouldn't shut up. They were respectful, but they just kept rambling!"

Answer: Similar to a traffic cop, try hand gestures. Try the hand up "halt" sign to politely indicate to a student to stop speaking while simultaneously pointing to another student, allowing him or her an opportunity to speak. It truly is like directing verbal traffic because you control the flow of communication.

Question: "During my counseling session, it became clear that there was one particular student who really had no right to be there. I soon discovered that he didn't even know the victim and was obviously looking for an excuse to get out of class.

The others students were aware of this and got upset. What should I have done?"

> **Answer:** The student should have been removed to prevent further disruption. To avoid embarrassment, the student could have been asked to step outside the room, informed of the situation, and then instructed to return to class (preferably with an escort to ensure that he or she did indeed return to class). Although this option would have interrupted the rhythm of the session, it's necessary because a larger disruption was occurring with the student remaining in the venue.

Question: "As I was conducting my session, I noticed that there were at least three kids who had legitimate issues that weren't even related to the loss of the student. I tried to track them down after the session, but before I got to them, they returned to their classes. What can I do to prevent this in the future?"

> **Answer:** Use a writing tablet to jot down the names of the students in the group. In addition to helping the counselor to remember names, it can also help to flag students who are at risk or in need of further support. It's important not to let a student whose emotional state necessitates additional intervention return to class. Interestingly, it's not unusual to have a student(s) attend a counseling session only to present issues that aren't actually related to the crisis situation.

Question: "After terminating my counseling session, three or four of the students kept wandering around the media center. They contributed during the session, but then gave every excuse not to return to class. At one point, one of them became disrespectful toward the librarian who had simply asked them why they hadn't returned to class. How could I have helped return these students to class without a hassle?"

> **Answer:** Simply approach the students and ask them if further support is necessary; however, don't offer a group session. Instead, offer to meet with them individually. This will immediately break up their group and the students likely will opt to return to class. Be sure to escort the students to their classrooms (this is a good opportunity for the group facilitator to take a brief break). If this isn't possible, ask another student or faculty member to escort them to their respective classrooms.

References

Adelman, H. S. (1996). Restructuring education support services and integrating community resources. *School Psychology Review, 25*(4), 431–445.

Adelman, H. S., & Taylor, L. (2006). *The implementation guide to student learning supports in the classroom and schoolwide: New directions for addressing barriers to learning.* Thousand Oaks, CA: Corwin Press.

Allen, M., Burt, K., Bryan, E., Carter, D., Orsi, R., & Durkin, L. (2002). School counselors' preparation for and participation in crisis intervention. *Professional School Counseling, 6*(2), 96–102.

Allen, M., Jerome, A., White, A., Marston, S., Lamb, S., Pope, D., & Rawlins, C. (2002). The preparation of school psychologists for crisis intervention. *Psychology in the Schools, 39*(4), 427–439.

Allen, M., Jerome, A., White, A, Pope, D., & Malinka, A. (2001). Effective university training for school crisis intervention. *Trainer's Forum, 21*, 1–3. Retrieved August 22, 2006, from http://trainersofschoolpsychologists.org

Ayalon, O. (1979). Community oriented preparation for emergency: C.O.P.E. *Death Education, 3*(4).

Ayalon. O. (1993). Post traumatic stress recovery. In J. Wilson & B. Raphael (Eds.), *International handbook of traumatic stress syndromes* (pp. 855–866). New York: Plenum.

Ayalon, O. (2005). Children's reactions to terrorism. In D. Knafo (Ed.), *Living with terror, working with trauma: Clinical handbook* (pp. 171–200). New York: Jason Aronson.

Basham, A., Appleton, V. E., & Dykeman, C. (2000). School crisis intervention: Building effective crisis management teams. *Counseling and Human Development, 33*(3), 1–8.

Brock, S. E., Lazarus, P. J., & Jimerson, S. R. (Eds.). (2002). *Best practices in school crisis prevention and intervention.* Bethesda, MD: National Association of School Psychologists.

Brock, S. E., Sandoval, J., & Lewis, S. (2001). *Preparing for crises in the schools: A manual for building school crisis response teams.* (2d ed.). New York: John Wiley.

Caplan, G. (1964). *Principles of preventive psychiatry.* New York: Basic Books.

Center for Mental Health in Schools at UCLA. (2005). *A resource aid packet on responding to a crisis at a school.* Los Angeles: Author. Retrieved August 22, 2006, from http://smhp.psych.ucla.edu

Chibarro, J. S., & Jackson, C. M. (2006). Helping students cope in the age of terrorism: Strategies for school counselors. *Professional School Counseling, 94,* 314–321.

Heath, M. A., & Sheen, D. (2005). *School-based crisis intervention: Preparing all personnel to assist.* New York: Guilford.

Jaksec, C. M. (2001). Common oversights during crisis intervention. *The School Administrator, 58*(1), 42.

Jaksec, C. M., Dedrick, R., & Weinberg, R. (2000). Classroom teachers' ratings of the acceptability of in-class crisis intervention services. *Traumatology, 6*(1), 1–16.

James, R. K., & Gilliland, B. E. (2004). *Crisis intervention strategies.* (5th ed.). Belmont, CA: Thomson Brooks/Cole.

Jimerson, S. R., Brock, S. E., & Pletcher, S. W. (2005). An integrated model of school crisis preparedness and intervention: A shared foundation to facilitate international crisis intervention. *School Psychology International, 26*(3), 275–296.

New York Study Center. (2006, August 22). *The mental health aftermath of Hurricane Katrina: How can we help children get back on their feet?* Retrieved August, 22, 2006, from http://www.AboutOur Kids.org.

Pines, M. (2001). The school crisis intervention team at work. *Internet Journal of Rescue and Disaster Medicine, 2*(2). Retrieved August 22, 2006, from http://www.ispub.com/ostia/index.php?xmlFile Path=journals/ijrdm/vol2n2/school.xml

Pitcher, G. D., & Poland, S. (1992). *Crisis intervention in the schools.* New York: Guilford.

Putin meets angry Beslan mothers. (2005, September 5). BBC News. Retrieved August 24, 2006, from http://news.bbc.co.uk/1/hi/ world/europe/4207112.stm

Pynoos, R. S., & Nader, K. (1988). Psychological first aid and treatment approach to children exposed to community violence: Research implications. *Journal of Traumatic Stress, 1,* 445–473.

Roberts, A. R. (Ed.). (2005). *Crisis intervention handbook: Assessment, treatment, and research* (3d ed.). Oxford and New York: Oxford University Press.

Sandoval, J. (Ed.). (2001). *Handbook of crisis counseling, intervention and prevention in the schools* (2d ed.). Mahwah, NJ: Lawrence Erlbaum.

Schonfeld, D. J., & Newgass, S. (2003). *Office for Victims of Crime bulletin: School crisis response initiative.* Washington, DC: U.S. Department of Justice. Retrieved August 22, 2006, from http://www.ojp.usdoj.gov/ovc/publications/bulletins/schoolcrisis/

Schonfeld, D. J., Kline, M., & Members of the Crisis Intervention Committee. (2005). School-based crisis intervention: An organizational model. In Center for Mental Health in Schools at UCLA, *A resource aid packet on responding to a crisis at a school.* Los Angeles: Author. Retrieved August 22, 2006, from http://smhp.psych.ucla.edu

School District of Volusia County. (2005). *Crisis intervention manual.* Volusia, FL: Author. Retrieved August 24, 2006, from http://www.volusia.k12.fl.us/curriculum/Manuals/crisis_manual.pdf

Zirkel, P. A., & Gluckman, I. B. (1996). Student suicide. *Principal, 75*(5), 45–46.

CORWIN
PRESS

The Corwin Press logo—a raven striding across an open book—represents the union of courage and learning. Corwin Press is committed to improving education for all learners by publishing books and other professional development resources for those serving the field of PreK–12 education. By providing practical, hands-on materials, Corwin Press continues to carry out the promise of its motto: **"Helping Educators Do Their Work Better."**